CAMBRIDGE LIBRARY COLLECTION

Books of enduring scholarly value

Classics

From the Renaissance to the nineteenth century, Latin and Greek were compulsory subjects in almost all European universities, and most early modern scholars published their research and conducted international correspondence in Latin. Latin had continued in use in Western Europe long after the fall of the Roman empire as the lingua franca of the educated classes and of law, diplomacy, religion and university teaching. The flight of Greek scholars to the West after the fall of Constantinople in 1453 gave impetus to the study of ancient Greek literature and the Greek New Testament. Eventually, just as nineteenth-century reforms of university curricula were beginning to erode this ascendancy, developments in textual criticism and linguistic analysis, and new ways of studying ancient societies, especially archaeology, led to renewed enthusiasm for the Classics. This collection offers works of criticism, interpretation and synthesis by the outstanding scholars of the nineteenth century.

Observations on the Topography of the Plain of Troy

James Rennell (1742–1830) could be claimed as the father of historical geography. After a long career at sea and in India, during which he had learned surveying and cartography, he returned to England and entered the circle of Sir Joseph Banks, who encouraged him to widen his interests to include the geography of the ancient world. In this work, published in 1814, Rennell compares the actual topography of the area in which Troy was believed to be located with the accounts of ancient commentators on Homer, with the Homeric accounts themselves, and finally with the work of ancient geographers. Without offering his own solution to the problem, he demolishes with zest the then current theory that Troy was located at the village of Bournabashi – a conclusion with which Heinrich Schliemann later agreed. Rennell's posthumously published work on the topography of Western Asia is also reissued in this series.

Cambridge University Press has long been a pioneer in the reissuing of out-of-print titles from its own backlist, producing digital reprints of books that are still sought after by scholars and students but could not be reprinted economically using traditional technology. The Cambridge Library Collection extends this activity to a wider range of books which are still of importance to researchers and professionals, either for the source material they contain, or as landmarks in the history of their academic discipline.

Drawing from the world-renowned collections in the Cambridge University Library and other partner libraries, and guided by the advice of experts in each subject area, Cambridge University Press is using state-of-the-art scanning machines in its own Printing House to capture the content of each book selected for inclusion. The files are processed to give a consistently clear, crisp image, and the books finished to the high quality standard for which the Press is recognised around the world. The latest print-on-demand technology ensures that the books will remain available indefinitely, and that orders for single or multiple copies can quickly be supplied.

The Cambridge Library Collection brings back to life books of enduring scholarly value (including out-of-copyright works originally issued by other publishers) across a wide range of disciplines in the humanities and social sciences and in science and technology.

Observations on the Topography of the Plain of Troy

And on the Principal Objects Within,
and Around it Described, or Alluded to, in the Iliad

JAMES RENNELL

CAMBRIDGE
UNIVERSITY PRESS

CAMBRIDGE
UNIVERSITY PRESS

University Printing House, Cambridge, CB2 8BS, United Kingdom

Cambridge University Press is part of the University of Cambridge.

It furthers the University's mission by disseminating knowledge in the pursuit of
education, learning and research at the highest international levels of excellence.

www.cambridge.org
Information on this title: www.cambridge.org/9781108071826

This edition first published 1814
This digitally printed version 2014

ISBN 978-1-108-07182-6 Paperback

OBSERVATIONS

ON THE

TOPOGRAPHY

OF THE

PLAIN OF TROY;

AND ON THE PRINCIPAL OBJECTS WITHIN, AND AROUND IT DESCRIBED, OR ALLUDED TO, IN THE

ILIAD.

SHEWING

That the SYSTEM of M. DE CHEVALIER, so long upheld, is founded on a MOST ERRONEOUS TOPOGRAPHY. And also, that the TWO SOURCES, denominated the WARM, and the COLD, SPRING, on which his System materially rests, DO NOT PRESENT ANY CONTRAST; but are EXACTLY ALIKE, in Point of TEMPERATURE; that is, COLD.

WITH A MAP,

In which the TOPOGRAPHY set forth by M. DE CHEVALIER, is contrasted with the several Statements of THREE OTHER TRAVELLERS in the TROAD. Also, a Sketch of the Western Part of the REGION of MOUNT IDA.

ʿουτως αταλαιπωρος τοις πολλοις ἡ ζητησις της αληθειας, και επι τα ἑτοιμα μαλλον τρεπονται.　　　　Thucydid. in Procem.

In the Investigation of Truth, most men are so sparing of labour, that they willingly embrace those opinions which most readily present themselves.　　(Dr. Gillies.)

BY JAMES RENNELL,

FELLOW OF THE ROYAL SOCIETIES OF LONDON, EDINBURGH, AND GOTTINGEN; AND MEMBER OF THE INSTITUTE OF PARIS.

LONDON:

PRINTED BY W. BULMER AND CO. CLEVELAND-ROW, ST. JAMES'S; AND SOLD BY G. & W. NICOL, BOOKSELLERS TO HIS MAJESTY, PALL-MALL.

1814.

PREFACE.

THE within Tract originally formed a part of a voluminous work, on the COMPARATIVE GEOGRAPHY (the Ancient with the Modern) of LOWER ASIA: the completion of which has been delayed, from various circumstances; amongst others, the expectation of receiving much additional and valuable matter. But as this portion of it (as well as some others) could be extracted, without violence, either to the general work, or to the extract itself; and as two respectable Travellers have very recently given their observations and opinions, and that in considerable detail, on the TOPOGRAPHY of the TROAD; this was judged to be a proper season for sending it forth: that is, whilst those who take an interest in matters of antiquity, might be supposed to have their attention drawn once more towards the subject. And more especially, since the opinion of one of the beforementioned travellers, has disturbed that long repose of the question, which M. de Chevalier's system seems to have produced.

[a] The TOPOGRAPHY of the PLAIN of TROY has become a kind of party question in literature: though by far the greater

What follows, is taken from the original manuscript, written in 1810, from Notes and Observations of a much earlier date.

number of persons have espoused the opinion of M. de Chevalier; or what, if the reader pleases, may be termed, THE
NEW DOCTRINE : for to that time (1791), a different opinion,
founded on the authority of those, who were deemed the best
informed amongst the Ancients, had prevailed.

Such being the state of things, it became a service of some
danger, for an humble individual to enter the lists, in the face
of an opinion, which had been repeatedly approved by men
of the first erudition in Europe, during the last twenty years:
but as it will be made to appear, that their opinions were
founded on an erroneous statement of the Topography, as
well as of the temperature of the Springs, (*absolutely* as well
as *comparatively*), the Author trusts that he will stand acquitted
of presumption, or of a wish to cavil.

It was, indeed, the wish of the Author, to keep aloof from
controversy: and for that reason, he had originally intended
to acquiesce in the system of M. de Chevalier. But finding,
subsequently, that the two sources, denominated the *warm*
and the *cold* Spring, were exactly of the same temperature; [b]
that instead of TWO, there were at least EIGHT of the same
kind; and also that Professor Carlyle had found a river (or
torrent) of the name of SHIMAR, in a position proper to
the SIMOÏS, (and which had escaped the observation of

[b] It is wonderful that so many persons of respectability, amongst those who
have visited the Springs, should have allowed themselves to be so far deceived,
as to report that one of them was *warm* and the other *cold*, when both were of a
like temperature.

Messrs. Chevalier, Kauffer, and Gell; [c]) the charm began to dissolve. Indeed, with M. de Chevalier for his guide, the Author had at times found, as he thought, reason to doubt the accuracy of the Poet: first, in the improbable extent of the ground, over which his heroes were represented to have marched and fought, within a given time; and secondly, for his want of exactness, in his descriptions and characters of the rivers of the *Troad;* since it was difficult to regard the *equable* and *smoothly flowing* River of BOUNARBASHI, as the *irregular* and *furious torrent* of the SCAMANDER. As the subject, therefore, fell within the scope of his work, his silence respecting it might either have been taken for a tacit approval of M. de Chevalier's system; or that, although he disapproved it, he still found the subject too difficult for him to attempt. Had the difference of opinion been in shades only, he would have remained silent: but it was total: in respect of the identity of the Rivers, and of the *Tumuli;* and the position of Troy. He therefore determined to seek a more probable developement of the scene of the Iliad, in the quarter where the Ancients, as well as the Moderns in general, to the time of M. de Chevalier, had placed it.

Mr. Gell, although amongst the supporters of M. de Chevalier's general system, has ventured to think for himself, in his mode of setting forth his assent to the identity of the rivers, and to the given position of Troy.[d] He has, indeed, done this

[c] As also (as appears by his second volume) of M. Choiseul Gouffier.

[d] In his very elegant work of the Topography of the Plain of Troy, 1804.

in such a manner, as to give an opponent fair play: and
instead of taking away the ground, on which alone the subject could be contested, he has even cleared it of the mountainous incumbrances laid on it, by the erroneous Topography
of M. de Chevalier: by which the detection of this gentleman's errors, has been hitherto prevented, by an absolute
removal of the means: that is, of the extensive Plain opened
to us by Mr. Gell, on the east of the River Mender. For,
in the Topography of M. de Chevalier, this space is, for the
most part, described as a mountainous region.

Hence Mr. Gell's conduct procures for him a distinction,
next to that of having accomplished his object, with the most
consummate success. For having given a more correct Topography; as well as a complete idea of the nature of the whole
ground of the Troad, by means of a set of *panoramic* landscapes; he has laid so ample and solid a foundation, that the
Author has been enabled to raise on it a superstructure, from
the materials furnished by Professor Carlyle. So that by the
aid of both sets of materials, combined, he has been able to
establish a new system: or rather to revert to the ancient
one, with an increased facility of explanation and proof.

It may possibly be objected, that the Author has entered
too much into detail; and often dwells on circumstances of
little moment: but as one principal object in view was to
endeavour to establish the *consistency of the story of the Poem*,
in what relates to the *Scene of Action*, and to the *Acts of the
Personages concerned;* considered as mere human agents; it

could no otherwise be accomplished, than by entering into detailed enquiries, and by a frequent use of hypotheses. Repetitions, also, were found to be unavoidable, in the attempt to render each separate head of enquiry more distinct.

The Author has, on a former occasion, declared his ignorance of the Greek language; [e] which has again rendered it necessary to have recourse to translations. On the present occasion, where the argument sometimes hangs on a doubtful, or at least, a disputed phraseology; and where all the descriptions are in *poetic language*, it may probably be concluded, not without reason, that the just mentioned deficiency on the part of the Author, is likely to be productive of still greater inconvenience, than on the former occasion.

But as it does not always happen, that a critical knowledge of languages, and a turn for disquisitions of this kind, meet in the same person; it may perhaps be allowed, that the sense of the text, as ascertained by able grammarians, or Philologers, may be used as a ground-work, by such as are qualified to pursue other necessary enquiries with effect. Nor will this argument lose a tittle of its force, should the public voice exclude the Author from this class of persons. The History of Editorship seems to prove that there are cases, in which all the learning of the scholar, has not rendered him equal to the task of elucidating his Author, when

In the Preface to the Geographical System of Herodotus, page ix. to which the Author begs leave to refer the Reader.

b

explanations have been attempted, in the usual manner, by the medium of notes. Or, in other words, that a scholar may be a most perfect judge of the beauty of Homer's poetry; but that, through the want, either of a more competent knowledge of nature; or of general, as well as of military, science, and practice, he may be incapable of illustrating certain parts of the Action of the Poem. For this Action will be found to bear the test of examination, in respect of its consistency, as far as human agency is concerned: and therefore is not to be regarded as a mere vehicle of poetical effusions; but rather as a consistent story, adorned with all the graces of Poetry.

The Author has been informed that the version of Mr. Cowper is, in general, very faithful; although for the present purpose, a more literal one would, perhaps, have been more useful. The Author ventured to trouble a friend for literal translations of certain passages, which were very important to his purpose: but the boundary of discretion was not to be transgressed, in order to obtain reputation, by the use of another's judgment.

Mr. Cowper's version has, accordingly, been followed generally. It appeared quite unnecessary to transcribe the numerous quotations from the original Greek, into the Memoir; since the class of readers who may wish to consult the original, are, most assuredly, in possession of a copy of it. It would moreover, have swelled the work unnecessarily, as well as enhanced its price.

References are constantly made to the numbers in the Greek original, as well as to those of the translation.

It remains that the Author should make his acknowledgments to his Friends, by whose assistance he has been enabled to render his Work more perfect.   He begs leave, therefore, to offer his best thanks to Sir Joseph Banks, Sir Charles Blagden, Dr. Gillies, Mr. Gell, Mr. John Hawkins, Mr. John Walker, Mr. Robert H. Inglis ; and to Messrs. Thomas and Philip Hope.   He laments that Professor Carlyle should not have lived to witness the great advantages derived from his valuable discovery of the upper course of the Shimar River; which particular, perhaps more than any other, has operated to *restore* the *Ancient System* of Topography of the Troad.

A general reference to Mr. Gell's Book, on the Topography of the Troad, and particularly to his Plans and Landscapes, will explain, most effectually, the ideas meant to be expressed by the matter of this Tract.

The Reader is also referred to Dr. Chandler's History of Troy, published in 1802, for a great number of curious and interesting particulars, respecting that city and territory. He appears to have collected together, all that is known on the subject.

CONTENTS.

SECTION III.

SECTION IV

NOTICES RESPECTING THE SEVERAL DIVISIONS OR COM-
PARTMENTS OF THE ANNEXED MAP.

THE accompanying Map, which is explanatory of the present subject, contains six compartments; of which, the
following is a short description and explanation.

N°. I, which is to be regarded as a document founded on
authority, has for its groundwork, the observations of Mr.
Gell, contained in his Book on the Topography of the
Troad; and in his Plan, N°. XLV. To these are added,
certain observations of Messrs. Kauffer and Carlyle: but
these contain a small proportion of the whole; since all the
matter, to the *left* of the *hair line* x x x is from Mr. Gell.
The part from M. Kauffer (See N°. IV.) consists of the outline of the Valley of Thymbrek, and the course of its River;
together with a portion of Mount *Ida*, contiguous to it.

The sketch of Professor Carlyle (N°. V.) furnishes the
routes from *Koum-kala*, through *In Tepé*, *Koum-kui*, *Thymbrek-kui*, and *Atchekui*, to *Bounarbashi*: together with the
course of the River Shimar, generally, from Mount *Ida* to
the sea.

The position of Troy is assumed, merely with a view to
aid the imagination, in the process of arranging the suite of
positions, given by Demetrius; and in reference to the
Tumulus taken for that of *Myrinna*. But it is by no means
pretended, to fix the exact site; although it is probable
that the *quarter* in which it stood, cannot be mistaken.

c

N°. II. is an attempt to reconcile the ancient topography of the fields of battle, the Grecian camp and wall, and the camp of the Trojans, near it; the sea coast of the Bay, between the Promontories of *Sigæum* and *Rhœteum;* and the lower courses of the *Scamander* and *Simoïs;* to the events related in the *Iliad.*

N°. III. is M. de Chevalier's Plain of Troy, reduced to one half of the original scale. It will there be seen, that instead of a wide Plain on the east of the Mender, between the opening of the Thymbrek Valley and Bounarbashi, he brings the hills very near to the bank of the Mender; whilst the Plain between the Rivers Mender and Bounarbashi, is widened far beyond the proportions given in the Plans of Mr. Gell and M. Kauffer.

The Reader is requested to compare this N°. III. of M. de Chevalier,[f] with M. Kauffer's, on the right, and Mr. Gell's on the left: as also to refer to the note in page 33, for Mr. Gell's statement of the extent of the Plain. It will appear, moreover, that the River Shimar is entirely omitted in N°. III.; and that the Thymbrek is substituted for it: whilst the *true place* of the Thymbrek, according to Messrs. Gell, Kauffer, and Carlyle, is filled up with hills. In effect, that the two Vallies are confounded together, and made into one. See N°. I. IV. and V.

N°. IV. is the Plan of M. Kauffer, made, as is said, at the instance of Count Ludolf. This copy of the original MS. Plan, was obligingly communicated by my friend, Mr. John

---

[f] In M. de Chevalier's Plan, although the *sites* of Kalifatli and Koumkui Villages, are inserted in their proper places, yet their *names* are omitted. In the annexed Map the omissions have been supplied.

Hawkins; who has himself traversed the ground,[g] and has no doubt of the authenticity of the Plan, from whence it was copied. It differs materially from the one published by Messrs. Clarke and Cripps, in 1803. Mr. Hawkins accounts for the differences amongst the several Plans, passing under the name of Kauffer, both from their being *copies* of *copies*, often carelessly made; and from the license taken by persons, to insert their own ideas; a glaring instance of which, in the copy of 1803, is pointed out by Mr. Hawkins and Mr. Gell: for the *marshy* ground between *Koumkala* and *In Tepé*, is there described as a *hilly* tract.

A second error of the same copy of 1803, is the narrowing of the Plain (almost to nothing) on the eastern side of the Mender, in the quarter towards Koum-kui, where, according to Mr. Gell, and M. Kauffer's original Map, it is more than a mile in breadth. It may be suspected that the distances in M. Kauffer's Plan, are generally too great.

But this Plan of M. Kauffer's (as well as that of Mr. Gell), entirely omits the tract between the Plain, east of the Mender, and the Vale of Thymbrek; whence it has happened, that the upper part of the course of the *Shimar*, or River of Kalifatli, has remained unknown: and the river was supposed to terminate (or rather to *originate*) at Chiblak: from which point, downwards to Kalifatli, they both describe it.[h]

[g] See the Edinburgh Phil. Trans. Vol. IV. Literary Class.

[h] Dr. Clarke, whose second volume has appeared since the above was written, has confirmed the important fact of the extension of the river that passes by Chiblak: that is, the *Shimar*. The Doctor names it from *Kalifatli*: but Mr. Carlyle, who, from his knowledge of Oriental languages, was enabled to enquire more particularly into the matter, calls it *Shimar*. The term *Osmak*, employed by Dr. Clarke, should probably have been *Irmak*, a Turkish name for river; so that it would be *Kalifatli River*.

N°. V. is a sketch by Professor Carlyle, reduced to about half the scale of the original.

This is, indeed, a very rude and imperfect performance, if considered as a piece of geography; to which, indeed, it has no title; being done merely to express the general direction of some important routes, which the minutes of the Journal alone, would not have accomplished. It is, however, highly valuable; as those routes very satisfactorily prove the existence and course of the River SHIMAR; the supposed SIMOÏS. Professor Carlyle has also pointed out its different courses in winter and in spring, or rather, in its swoln, and in its low state. In the former, it joins the Mender at Kali-fatli; in the latter, near Koum-kala; passing in its course by Koum-kui; at which place, one of the copies of M. Kauffer's Map, notes the junction of *a* river with the Thym-brek; and which is, doubtless, the Shimar in question. On its junction, it communicates its name to the Thymbrek; being the larger stream, according to Mr. Carlyle. It is worthy of remark, that in the accompanying Map, by M. Kauffer, there is the *trace,* as of an ancient water-course, from the quarter of Koum-kui, to the inlet named *In Tepé,* answering to the ancient course of the *Scamander,* accord-ing to Pliny's description. (lib. v. c. 30.) [i]

It was on occasion of the discovery of the course of the Shimar River, by Mr. Carlyle; and the exposure of the wide Plain, east of the Mender, by Mr. Gell (for the cor-rected copy of M. Kauffer's Plan had not then made its

---

The Reader is cautioned not to confound Koum-*kui* with Koum-*kala.* The former is a village, near the opening of the Valley of Thymbrek: the other, the town belonging to the castle, at the southern point of the entrance of the Darda-nelles. One is Sand *Village;* the other Sand *Castle.*

appearance); that the Author was enabled to discuss, with any effect, the subject of the following Memoir. Thus, Mr. Carlyle proves the existence of *two* rivers, within the space in which M. Chevalier describes *one* only.[k]

[k] It may be satisfactory to the Reader, to compare the minutes of the Professor's Journal, between the Dardanelles and Bounarbashi, with the ground in his sketch, &c.

H	M.	
		March 9.
9	6	Left *Yenishehr;* crossed the *Mender,* and soon after the
		Shimar: i. e. the united streams of the *Shimar* and *Tymbrek:* but which, after their junction, takes its name from the larger stream.
		Crossed the *Touzla Azma,* or Salt Stream.
		Crossed another salt stream, named *In Tepé Azma.*
		In Tepé, (Tumulus of *Ajax.*)
11	48	Left *In Tepé.*
12	7	Entered the Plain.
—	17	Cross the *Shimar:* and arrive at *Koum-kui.*
1	30	Left *Koum-kui.*
2	20	*Khalili-kui.*
4	30	Left *Khalili,* and soon afterwards crossed the *Tymbrek* River.
5	30	Village of *Tymbrek.*
		March 10.
8	30	Left *Tymbrek-kui,* and proceeded in a south-westerly direction to
9	30	*Eski-Akshi-kui;* which lies about half an hour's distance from the *Tymbrek.*
11	11	Left E. A. K., and proceeded nearly E. b. S. till we arrived at the banks of
11	38	The River *Shimar.*
12	12	To a ruined Aqueduct over the *Shimar.**
—	—	Returned to Eski-Akshi-kui.
2	40	Left E. A. K. again.
3	6	*Mal Tepé* on the right.
3	20	*Akshi-kui.*
3	27	*Khana Tepé* on the left. Another *Tepé* or *Tumulus* on the right: the road passes between them.
3	45	Crossed the *Mender* River.
4	25	*Bounarbashi* Village.

The time is omitted throughout.

It is noted on the original sketch, that the bearing along the upper part of the course of the Shimar River, is *nearly* E. b. S. But it is *laid down on the sketch,* about SE. b. E. It then becomes a question, which of the two is right? It might have been expected, that the act of constructing the Map, from the Notes, would have sufficiently awakened the recollection of the Traveller The Author has followed the Note. Had the Sketch been followed, the hill of Atchekui would have stood very much nearer to the Shimar River. (See p. 46.)

N°. VI. contains a general view of the positions and directions of the principal chains of Mount Ida : as also the course of the Mender, taken for the *Scamander* of Demetrius, from Mount *Cotylus*. By this is also shewn, the particular chain of Ida, intended by Strabo, Herodotus, and Xenophon : and which appears to be distinct from that, which according to Demetrius, contains the sources of the *Scamander*, *Æsepus*, and *Granicus*.

This compartment is a small portion of an unpublished Map of *Æolis*, *Ionia*, the *Hellespont*, &c. on an enlarged scale.

*   *   *   *   *

The whole interval of time employed in the ILIAD, appears to have been about fifty-seven days : and that portion of it, between the first battle, before the *Scæan* Gate, and the death of Hector, eight days only ; both inclusive.

ERRATA.

Those marked * affect the sense.

* Page 14, line the last, for *monuments*, read *objects*.
     * 25, line 20, read, *a river whose principal sources are from the north-east.*
     * 27, line 20, r. *hill of Atchekui.*
     * 32, near the bottom, r. (*Mr. Hawkins and Mr. Gell excepted.*
     33, line 7, r. *of their judging aright.*
     43, line 16, r. *from what happens to other rivers.*
     * 44, line 13, dele *both.*
     * 46, note, r. *as far, or farther.*
     58, line the last, after Mender, add, *which therefore ought to be the Scamander.*
     59, line 18, r. *to the place of the conflux.*
     * 60, line 5, from bottom, for *none*, read *few.*
     66, line 4, r. *and that is.*
         line 7, refers to the note (s)
         line 10, See Mr. Gell's Troy, page 74.
     * 75, line 4, read *descriptions.*
         15, read, *and approaching within 8½ stade?*
     85, line 19, put a (?).
     88, line 18, part of the parenthesis wanting.
     97, line 4, from bottom, read 43.
     101, line 3, read, *in a similar position.*
     * 112, note, for *beech trees*, read *wild fig trees.*
     * 133, note, last line, read *for.*

PART I.

CONTAINING A COMPARISON OF THE IDEAS OF THE ANCIENT
GEOGRAPHERS; AND OF DEMETRIUS OF SCEPSIS IN
PARTICULAR; WITH THE ACTUAL TOPOGRAPHY
OF THE TROAD.

OBSERVATIONS, &c.

PART I.

SECTION I. PRELIMINARY OBSERVATIONS.

*Prevailing Ideas respecting the Topography of the Troad—
The Site decisively marked, by the Promontories, and the
River's Mouth. — The System of M. de Chevalier, founded
on an erroneous Topography—Demetrius of Scepsis, approved by Strabo—by M. Heyne, and by Dr. Chandler—
discredited by M. de Chevalier—Misapprehensions respecting
the Source of the Scamander, the great Cause of difficulty,
hitherto, in developing the Subject—The hot Spring before
the Scæan Gate not to be found—The Ancients believed the
general Truth of the Story of the Iliad :—but the question
here, is only whether Homer's Description agrees with the
reputed site—Curiosity both of Ancients and Moderns respecting the Site and Remains of Troy—The Subject to be
investigated, by comparing the Ancient Descriptions, with the
actual Topography—Proposed manner and order of treating
the Subject.*

THE scene of the warfare of the ILIAD is well known to
have been described by the poet, as an extensive plain, or
flat valley ; intersected by two torrent streams from MOUNT
IDA ; and which, forming a junction in that plain, discharged

their confluent waters into the *Hellespont*, between two promontories; which, although *spoken of* by Homer,[a] are not *named* by him: but from succeeding authorities,[b] are well known to have been intended for those of *Sigæum* and *Rhoeteum*. They are, moreover, strongly marked by the positions of the *tumuli*, ascribed to Achilles and Ajax, in reference to their military stations, in the line. These promontories, therefore, together with the discharge of the confluent waters, from *Ida*, by an opening situated between them, are unerring guides to the Plain of Troy; since there is *no other* river, or plain, that opens to the *Hellespont*, from Ida: so that it appears impossible to refer the scene of the Iliad, to any other spot, in the LESSER PHRYGIA.

It is also well known that one of those streams was named *Scamander* (or *Xanthus*); the other *Simoïs;* and that no others are mentioned by Homer. But a *third*, under the name of *Thymbrius*, is mentioned by Strabo, issuing from the valley of *Thymbra;* which valley (though not the river) is noticed by Homer.[c] And a *fourth* river, the *Bounarbashi*, appears not to have been mentioned by any of the ancients; unless it be the *Amnis navigabilis* of Pliny: which, however, is uncertain. At present, this river flows into the *Ægean* Sea, (or Archipelago); though appearances authorize a belief that at some period it ran into the *Hellespont;* either in a separate stream, or conjointly with the Mender; and that it was *forced* into its present channel, by an artificial mound, in order to irrigate the valley that branches off, from that of

---

[a] Iliad, lib. xiv. v. 36. Cowper, v. 42.   Pliny, in particular, lib. v. c. 30.

[c] In this valley was situated the Temple of Apollo, which doubtless gave him the name of *Thymbræus.*

Troy, between Erkessi-kui and Jeni-kui. (See the map, compartments N^{os}. I. and II.) Whether this change was effected
before, or after, the war of Troy, cannot be known: but in
the present enquiry, it may be fair to consider it, as being
posterior to that event.

Accordingly, there are *four* streams to be considered in
the Troad: *three* of which, that is, the *Mender, Shimar,* and
Thymbrek, in the present times, discharge themselves, in a
collective stream, into the Hellespont, (or Dardanelles);
and the *fourth,* the *Bounarbashi,* into the Archipelago. And
of these FOUR streams, THREE have by different writers
been severally taken for the *Simoïs,* and as many for the
Scamander.

But, in every system adopted for the arrangement of the
rivers of the Troad, the MENDER has always been regarded
as ONE of the TWO rivers that bounded the Trojan Plain:
(that is, it was supposed to be either the *Scamander,* or the
Simoïs: for it has been taken for both, in turn): and the
dispute is reduced simply to this: " on WHICH SIDE of the
Mender did the Plain of Troy lie?" The difference, at first
sight, appears trifling: but the circumstances belonging to
each of the systems, respectively, are very different indeed:
and thence require much discussion. M. de Chevalier's
system takes the *Mender* for the *Simoïs,* and the *Bounarbashi*
for the *Scamander;* whilst we regard the Mender as the
Scamander, leaving the Bounarbashi out of the question:
and seek, with Demetrius of *Scepsis,*[d] for a *Simoïs,* on the
opposite, or *eastern* side of the Mender. Our dissent from
the opinion of M. de Chevalier, is *chiefly* grounded on the

---

[d] An ancient city of *Troas,* situated *within* the western chain of *Mount Ida.*

accordance, in point of character and description, of the Mender, with the Scamander of Homer; and the total want of accordance in the Bounarbashi.

The system of M. de Chevalier is founded on a *most erroneous* topography; in which, not only the *principal part* of the *extensive plain*, lying on the east of the Mender, is converted into a *hilly tract;* but *a. river* and *its valley* are entirely omitted ; and *others* of a *different name* substituted for them. And it is the river *so omitted*, that appears to have constituted the *Simoïs* of DEMETRIUS; as the plain, *so filled up,* is HIS Plain of Troy ! After this, it becomes no matter of surprize, that M. de Chevalier should wish to under-rate the authority of Demetrius; so as scarcely to allow him to possess the ability of identifying a river, or a plain, even in the neighbourhood of his own residence. The reader is requested to compare the plan of M. de Chevalier, Nº. III. with those of Mr. Gell, and Mr. Kauffer; and with Mr. Carlyle's sketch; Nᵒˢ. I. IV. and V. in the annexed map.

But let it be enquired, what was the opinion of STRABO, a person who had well considered the authority of Demetrius.

He says, (page 603,) " I think we ought *generally to rely* " on the authority of Demetrius; a man of knowledge, and " so enthusiastically fond of Homer, as to have written 30 " books on about 60 lines of Homer's catalogue of the " Trojan forces.'ᵉ

The opinions of certain modern authors, of great respectability, are no less in favour of Demetrius.

He was cotemporary with SCIPIO AFRICANUS, who visited the Troad, B. C. 190.

The celebrated M. Heyne of Gottingen (in the Edinb.
Trans. Vol. iv. p. 76. Lit. Class) says :

" Demetrius seems indeed to have a just title to belief
" and respect, as he was born in the neighbourhood of the
" Troad ; and had, in all probability, surveyed it himself.
" Our good opinion of him is confirmed, by the accuracy
" with which particular places are laid down ; and by their
" coincidence with the descriptions of ancient poets.

" This author, however, gives rise to a still greater em-
" barassment, not so much respecting the situation of Troy ;
" *for it is assigned to what, in all probability, is its exact place ;*
" as in regard to the river *Scamander,* and its sources, which
" are thrown far back in the mountainous region behind
" Troy."[f]

And Dr. Chandler (Hist. Troy, pages 1. and 52,) says,
" He (Demetrius) was a great philologist and grammarian ;
" of high reputation for learning: and especially noted for
" his study of Homer, and his topographical commentaries
" on the Ilias.—His curious researches give him a just title
" to be mentioned always with respect."

After this, let the reader compare the style of M. Chevalier's criticisms, with that of the above testimonials. After
mentioning the attempt of Strabo to reconcile Demetrius
with Homer, on the subject of the fountains, attributed to
the Scamander, in the plain ; he says, (Plain of Troy, English
Transl. p. 59), " This is certainly a very obscure and unsatis-
" factory explication: and Demetrius and Strabo are *equally*
censurable, the one for his *negligence* in *committing* the

[f] It will, however, appear in the sequel, that the *Scamander* springs from
mountains that are far removed from Troy.

" *blunder;* and the other for adopting it, and endeavouring
" to give it authenticity."

Such is the modesty of the Gentleman, who produces
an erroneous map, to prove his own system, in contradiction
to Demetrius; whilst the latter was doubtless in the right.
The remaining part of the chapter is equally censurable, for
want of decorum; as well in the mode of speaking of *himself,*
as of the two ancient authors: even on a supposition that
he had himself been in the right.

In effect, Demetrius is slighted only by *those,* who could
not make his system square with *theirs;* although such
systems may have been founded on deficient information, or
on misconception.

It seems to be acknowledged on all hands, that the *place*
of the *source* of the *Scamander* is the great *stumbling block* to
the interpreters of the ILIAD; owing to the different modes
of translating the description of the two springs before the
Scæan Gate. (Iliad, xxii. v. 148.) Some have supposed it to
intend " *The sources* WHICH SUPPLIED the *Scamander;*"
whilst others have translated it " *Springs* OF THE *Scamander;*"
as appertaining to that river, either from their effecting a
junction with it, or from the notion that they were derived
from it. So that, perhaps, they ought rather to have been
denominated ADJUNCT STREAMS TO the Scamander, than
the REMOTE SOURCES, or HEADS of that river.

Moreover, Homer says elsewhere, that the *Scamander*
" *descends from the Idæan heights.*"⁵ Demetrius, who certainly did not refer the two springs of Homer, to those of
Bounarbashi (as he placed Troy in so different a position),

⁵ Iliad, lib. xii, v. 19. Cowper, v. 23.

derives the Scamander from *Mount Cotylus,* in the eastern chain of Ida : and is silent in respect of any of its sources in the plain. Hence one may conclude, that he understood the passage in Homer to mean nothing more than two *adjunct streams* to the Scamander; and not its *sources.*

Strabo, who follows him so far as to believe that " its source " was not in the plain, but in the mountain ;" accounts, in a most extraordinary manner, for the existence of the *cold* spring, (for no hot spring could then be found.) For he supposes it to be a portion of the water of the Scamander, forcing its way through a subterraneous channel, and again rising up to the surface of the ground.[h] This, at least, proves, that Strabo believed the source of the *main* river, to be *remote* from Troy : and at the same time, seems to shew how much the text of Homer, in this place, had perplexed him.

Homer surely had Mount *Cotylus* (that is *Gargarus*) in view, when he characterizes *Ida*[i] as abounding with springs ;[k]

---

[h] Page 602. By this we learn that either Demetrius, or Strabo, had recognised a cold spring, in a situation which *they thought* was *proper* to the celebrated springs of Homer. So that travellers should enquire after it ; as it might lead to some discovery.

There appears to be a difference of opinion, amongst the learned, whether Strabo ever visited the Troad in person. It seems probable, that he only sailed along the coast, from *Lectum,* and viewed the plain, rivers, and mountains, from *Sigæum,* or from the tumulus of Antilochus : as most of our modern travellers have done. Consequently, he must have derived the greater part of his information from the observations of others ; and it is probable that the writings **of** Demetrius, " *the Field of Troy,*" furnished all that relates to the interior of *Troas, Carasena,* &c. in the work of Strabo.

[i] See the map, compartment N°. VI.

[k] " *Spring-fed* Ida, mother of wild beasts." Iliad, lib. viii. v. 47. Cowper, v. 52. " Ida's mount with *rilling waters* veined." xiv. v. 283. Cowper, v. 332. and, again, v. 307. Cowper, 387. A number of sources descend from *Gargarus.*

because it suits that mountain, perfectly, but not the one opposite to the Trojan Plain, and to Bounarbashi; it having no *known* sources in it. Consequently, he can only be supposed to derive the *Scamander* from *Gargarus*.

With respect to the warm spring itself, as Demetrius could not find it, it would surely be vain for any one at present to attempt it: since he had, doubtless, opportunities of examining the ground in a closer and better manner than any one of our modern travellers could have done. It is a region subject to great earthquakes, the effects of some of which are on record. A spring of any kind is easily destroyed by such a convulsion: besides which, the changes that have probably taken place, during the lapse of ages, since the time of Homer, must be taken into the account.

———————

There can be no doubt that the Ancients believed the war of Troy to have happened; as they speak of it as of an acknowledged fact in history: but then, they of course made a distinction between history and heroic poetry: and no more believed that Vulcan dried up the waters of the *Scamander* to please Thetis, than we, that the Duke of Marlborough's victory of Blenheim " swelled the Danube with floods of gore, which fell from the vanquished."[1] But, in effect, whether Homer adopted for the subject of his poem a *real event of history*, (as we certainly conceive he did), or invented a *fiction* for it, is not the point to be considered in this place; but whether his description of the scene of

[1] Addison's Campaign.

action, agrees with the site acknowledged by the Ancients to be intended for it.[m]

It is well known that Herodotus, Thucydides, and the historians of Alexander, have all spoken of the Trojan war as a matter of real history. But the statements and arguments of Thucydides are most to the point, in proof of the general belief of the Ancients, concerning it : for he reasons on it as on any other historical fact. It may not be amiss, in this place, to quote some of his opinions and observations on the subject. (Peloponnesian War, lib. I.)

" Their power (that is, of the Greeks) by these methods gradually advancing, they were enabled, in process of time, to undertake the Trojan expedition." ————————————

" It is farther my opinion, that the assemblage of that armament, by Agamemnon, was not owing so much to the attendance of the suitors of Helen, in pursuance of the oath they had sworn to Tyndarus, as to his own superior power."— —" To these enlargements of power, Agamemnon succeeding, and being also superior to the rest of his countrymen, in naval strength, he was enabled, in my opinion, to form that expedition more from awe, than favour. It is plain that he equipped out the largest number of ships himself, besides those he lent to the Arcadians." ————————————

—" We ought not therefore to be incredulous, nor so much to regard the appearance of cities, as their power; and of course, to conclude the armament against Troy, to have been greater than ever was known before ; but inferior to

———
[m] Of those who have reported, on the subject of the Troad, Demetrius of *Scepsis* is the only one whose observations in *detail*, (preserved by Strabo,) have reached us : for those of Pliny, &c. apply to particular circumstances only.

those of our age.ᵃ And whatever credit be given to the
poetry of Homer in this respect, who no doubt as a poet
hath set it off with all possible enlargement, yet even, according to his account, it appeareth inferior." ——————
—"On their first landing they got the better in fight; the
proof is, that they could not otherwise have fortified their
camp with a wall.   Neither doth it appear that they exerted
all their strength at once; numbers being detached for supplies of provisions; to till the Chersonesus; and to forage
at large.   Thus divided as they were, the Trojans were
better able to make a ten years' resistance, being equal in
force to those who were at any time left to carry on the
siege.—In fact, they did not ply the work with all their
number, but only with a part constantly reserved for the
purpose : had they formed the siege with their whole force,
in less time, and with less difficulty, they must have taken
Troy."ᵇ

   Herodotus (in Euterpe, c. 113. *et seq.*) gives the answers of
the Ægyptian priests, to his enquiries respecting Helen.
They reported that Paris and Helen had arrived at a port
of the Nile, in their way from *Sparta* to *Troy;* and that the
King of Ægypt detained Helen, and the treasures plundered
from her husband; but expelled Paris, as an infamous person. The result of these enquiries tends to shew, that although
Troy was besieged and taken by the Greeks, yet that Helen
(of course) was not found there. The father of history remarks, (ch. 118.) that " this circumstance could not be

   ᵃ Alluding to the Peloponnesian war.
   ᵇ Dr. Smith's translation of Thucydides, Vol. I. pages 7, 8, 9, 10; edition
of 1812. The Trojan war is again mentioned in lib. ii, regarding *Amphilochus.*

unknown to Homer; but as he thought it less ornamental to his poem, he forbore to use it. That he did know it, is evident from that part of the Iliad, where he describes the voyage of Paris—who after various wanderings, at length arrived at *Sidon* in *Phœnicia* "[p]

Herodotus concludes this subject by remarking, that the restoration of Helen was not in the power of the Trojans; and that the Greeks placed no dependance on their assertions, which were indisputably true: " but all this (says he) with the subsequent destruction of Troy, might be ordained by Providence, to instruct mankind that the Gods proportioned punishments to crimes." (Euterpe, c. 120. Mr. Beloe's translation.)

One cannot be otherwise than surprized, that any learned person should *altogether* slight these testimonies; so as even to doubt the existence of Troy itself: unless, indeed, he disbelieved the truth of ancient history generally.

The verses of the ILIAD, ever in the mouths of the Greeks, kept alive the remembrance of the events which they recorded; whilst the *tumuli*, dispersed over and about the plain of Troy, gave a character of reality to the scene of warfare, which the mere natural scenery of mountains, promontories, and rivers, though described ever so characteristically in the poem, could not of themselves, perhaps, have

[p] Iliad, lib. vi. v. 290 *et seq.*

——————— " There stor'd she kept
Her mantles of all hues, accomplish'd works
Of fair *Sidonians* wafted o'er the deep
By godlike Paris, when the gallies brought
The high-born Helen to the shores of Troy." Cowper, v. 326 *et seq.*

effected : so that the Ancients never lost sight of the subject. The Greeks and Ionians who were in the habit of visiting, or passing in view of the spot, on commercial, or other errands, had their curiosity awakened by these monuments, which forced themselves on their notice; as well by their geographical position, as by their artificial form and bulk. The Macedonian dynasties which were afterwards established in Asia, by their founding the city of *Alexandria Troas,* still kept alive the memory of the events: and finally, the Romans, warmed by the fictitious story of their origin, adopted the inhabitants of the Troad for brethren; and consequently interested themselves deeply in all that concerned the Troad.

From these circumstances taken together, the curiosity of the Greeks and Romans led them to collect the traditions still existing: and to examine the ground, with a view to refer to it the transactions recorded in the Iliad : and surely no poem ever interested mankind so much, and during so long a continuance.

These enquiries had the effect of impressing a firm belief, on the minds of the enquirers, that Homer's story had truth for its basis : each tumulus, as we learn from Demetrius, being appropriated to its proper hero: the rivers which bounded the " *deathless Plain,*" being also discriminated ; as well as the bay and promontories, which marked the camp of the Greeks ; the Vale of *Thymbra,* and the chain of Mount *Ida.*q But the *precise site* of Troy was still unknown

q For instance, Pliny mentions, lib. xvi. c. 44, incidentally, the barrow or tumulus of ILUS, which had trees growing on, or about it ; and which probably he might have seen in his way through the *Troad.*

to Demetrius, although belief had attached itself to a particular spot: for the very ruins themselves being supposed to have perished,[r] nothing that was sufficiently marked, remained for the judgment to fix on. It is most probable that the materials of the city had been removed: perhaps to *New Ilium* and *Alexandria Troas*, which were built long before Demetrius or Lucan wrote. But in the time of Alexander, and before the building of the latter of those cities, it is probable that enough of the ruins of ancient Troy remained to direct him to the spot: so that the report of its general site may well have been handed down to the time of Demetrius; an interval of no more than 150 years, at most.[s] It appears certain, that even those who resided near the spot, about the time of Augustus, had lost all idea of the exact position, otherwise than by report; and the warm spring was absolutely unknown to Demetrius, nearly two centuries before our æra.

Nor have the moderns shewn less curiosity or industry than the ancients: but, obviously, they have pursued their object with fewer advantages. For many of the notices possessed by the ancients, must, of necessity, have been lost: and the severe restraints so long imposed by bigotry and tyranny, must have damped the spirit of enquiry; not to mention that the aspect of an inhabited and cultivated country, is continually changing. And although in

---

———— *etiam periére ruinæ*. (*Lucan's Pharsalia*, lib. ix.)

[s] Although the *city* visited by Alexander was that of *New Ilium* (Strabo, page 593), yet we may conclude that he also visited the site of the ancient city: for unless he had gone over the whole scene of the Iliad, he could not have been so well qualified to decide on the merits of the historical and descriptive parts of the poem.

latter times, the restraints have been generally removed ; yet, it has unfortunately happened, that a particular traveller (M. de Chevalier) having formed a system of his own, (plausible only from the erroneous statement of its topography, and of its hot and cold springs), nearly all of the succeeding travellers have confined themselves to his path, as if the question was set for ever *at rest ;* instead of extending their researches to quarters not yet sufficiently explored.

Now, although every one reads the Iliad as a poetical romance, in respect of its machinery of deities, &c. yet he may believe, that, as it relates to the mere actions of men, the foundation of the story may be generally true, howsoever embellished : and such readers will, no doubt, be gratified to find, that so many of the descriptions in Homer agree with the ground itself. But it is unfortunate, that the ancient description of the landscape is too general ; and that our present knowledge of it is less extensive than could be wished.

In order to make a just comparison of the description of the field of action of the Iliad (according to the scanty notices in Homer) with the actual topography, as far as the present state of our information goes; it becomes necessary, first, to enquire what were the ideas of the people, who lived and wrote at a period much nearer the date of the transactions ; that is, Demetrius of Scepsis, Strabo, and Pliny ; but more particularly of the former : and then to examine, how far the ground described by Demetrius, and referred to the present topography of the Troad, agrees with the notices in Homer. For, as Demetrius found the principal monuments described by Homer, whether natural or artificial, still in existence, one may be satisfied that those descriptions were real: and that although we have not been able to discover all those monuments, yet that they did once exist, and may even exist at present, although they may have escaped our research. Therefore, by the intermediate assistance of Demetrius, more facts may perhaps be verified.

The including ridges of hills, and the rivers, as well as the greater part of the *tumuli*, are still recognised; and the record concerning them is clear and distinct. Nothing more therefore seems to be required, than an unbiassed interpretation of the text of the poem, and a reference to a more accurate topography: the application will then, it is presumed, appear perfectly clear and natural.

In the course of the disquisition, it is proposed to treat the subject in the following manner and order:

FIRST, to compare the ideas of the ancient geographers, and particularly those of Demetrius, with the actual geography.

SECONDLY, to enquire how far the descriptions in Homer, can be reconciled to Demetrius, and to the actual geography.

And LASTLY, what is to be collected from the ancients, respecting the position of the ancient City of Troy itself.

But in order to understand with more effect the descriptions given by Demetrius, whether quoted directly from him by Strabo; or presumed to be derived from him, and occurring in various passages of the same author; it becomes previously necessary to give a general idea of MOUNT IDA itself: since the chains of hills that encompass the Plain of Troy, and the whole scene of the Iliad, *originate in,* or are *connected with,* Ida. And moreover, because the *largest* of the rivers, the *Scamander,* springs from the *most distant* range of Ida : thereby furnishing the direct means of discriminating it from the *other* rivers of the Troad, which spring from the ridge of Ida, nearest to the Plain of Troy.

SECTION II.

CONCERNING THE REGION OF MOUNT IDA.

IDA, *a Region composed of three principal Ranges of Moun-*
tains; Gargarus; *the* Trojan; *and* Lectum—*The second,*
which faces the Plain *of* Troy, *has been commonly regarded*
as the great body *of Ida, both by the Ancients and Moderns*
—*Path of Juno*—*Strabo misapprehended the Subject of Ida,*
and the Courses of its Rivers, in the Report of Demetrius of
Scepsis—Palæ Scepsis, Ænea, Polichna—Scepsis—*Ho-*
mer's Idea of Ida, appears to be correct—*The Mountain*
of Gargarus, *the same with* Cotylus — *Gives rise to the*
Scamander, Esepus, Granicus, &c.—*Dr. Pocock's Idea of*
Ida, *correct*—*M. D'Anville's the contrary.*

IDA, as we collect from Homer,[t] is not merely a mountain,
or even a single chain of mountains, but a *mountainous*
region; extending, in its greatest length, from the Promontory
of *Lectum* to *Zeleia* (that is from Cape Baba to Biga); and
in breadth, from the *Hellespont* to the neighbourhood of
Adramyttium : so that it occupied, by its ridges and ramifi-
cations, the whole of the tract anciently called the LESSER
PHRYGIA.[u]

Amongst a number of ridges or ranges, and irregular

[t] Iliad, lib. ii. v. 824. Cowper, v. 954 : xii. v. 19. Cowper, v. 23 : &c. &c.
[u] See the Map, N°. VI. The extent of Ida, from C. Baba to Biga, N E.-ward,
is 80 G. miles : and in breadth, rom N W. to S E. 30.

masses of mountains, of which it is composed, there are three ridges that are superior, in point of elevation, to the rest: and one of them eminently so. From their relative positions to each other, they may be compared, collectively, in point of form, to the Greek *Delta ;* the head, or northern-most angle of which approaches the Hellespont, near the site of the ancient *Dardanus;* and the two lower angles approach the promontory of *Lectum* on the one hand; *Adramyttium* on the other.

The loftiest of these ridges, is that which forms the right, or eastern side of the ∆; extending S E.-ward, between the Hellespont, and the head of the Gulf of *Adramyttium,*[x] and terminating in the lofty summit of *Gargarus;* called also, indifferently, *Cotylus;* and *Alexandrea;* and which over-tops, in every distant view, the great body of Ida, like a dome over the body of a temple.[y]

The SECOND ridge, forming the left of the ∆, runs parallel to the coast of the *Ægean* Sea, from N. to S. at the distance of six or seven miles. Its commencement in the north, is, like that of the former, near the Hellespont; and it extends far on, *towards* the Promontory of Lectum. In a general view from the west (See Mr. Gell's View, N°· XIX), it appears to extend *to* the promontory itself; although in reality it is separated from it by a wide valley, through which flows the Touzla, or Salt River.[z]

---

[x] Called also the *Idæan Bay.*

[y] See Mr. Gell's beautiful and characteristic views, in his Troy, N°s. XII. and XIX. The modern name of *Gargarus,* is *Kas-dagh.*

Strabo mentions (page 605) the *Saline* of *Tragesæa,* near *Hamaxytus,* on the coast of Troas. This is, no doubt, the one now in use, at the mouth of

The THIRD ridge, forming the base of the △, extends along the southern coast of the *Lesser Phrygia*, from the summit of Mount *Gargarus*, to the Promontory of *Lectum*; diminishing in altitude as it proceeds towards the latter (which Homer describes as the terminating point of Ida, on that side) [a] and which is, doubtless, the course of Juno, as described by him, in the same place. Mr. Hawkins says, that this ridge is not inferior in height to that which faces the Plain of Troy.

To prevent confusion, it becomes necessary to distinguish each of these ridges, by a particular name; and that of GARGARUS being already appropriated to the one which contains the peak of that name, it may perhaps be allowed to name the one that faces the Plain of Troy, and seems to appertain to it, in respect of *juxta-position* and *connexion*, the TROJAN IDA: and that which extends from *Gargarus* to *Lectum*, IDA LECTUM. The Author is aware that the western ridge has already been called, by some, *Ida Lectum*; but it being *separated* from the promontory, as before said; whilst the other is *continuous*, the whole way from the summit of *Gargarus*; and as it appears, moreover, to be the *poetical path* of Juno, under which consideration it has *an immediate reference* to LECTUM; there may perhaps be a propriety in calling this southern ridge by that name. If this be admitted, the three ridges, the eastern, western, and

the Touzla River, a league to the southward of *Alexandria Troas*. The agency of the *Etesian* winds, so oddly described by Strabo, was doubtless nothing more than that of raising the level of the sea, so as to overflow the margin, and fill the hollow plain within; where, in due time, it chrystallizes. (See Map, N°.VI.)

[a] Iliad xiv. v. 284 : Cowper, v. 333.

southern, will be respectively distinguished by the names of GARGARUS, The TROJAN, and LECTUM.[b]

Some of the most respectable authorities amongst the Ancients, and still more amongst the Moderns, have regarded the western range, or that over *Troy* and *Alexandria Troas*, as the *true* and *only* Ida; or they may have added to it a portion of the southern range. This idea was probably taken up from a view of the mountains from the side of Troy, and of the coast opposite to it; or from the Hellespont: from which quarters, it was most frequently viewed; and from whence the whole appears as one range; the nearest hiding the others; save only the Peak of *Gargarus*, which ordinarily passes for a distinct mountain, unconnected with Ida.

Herodotus, Xenophon, and Strabo, evidently design by

[b] *Lectum* and *Gargarus* are clearly discriminated in the XIVth Book of the Iliad, v. 284, *et seq*. (Cowper, v. 333) on occasion of the ascent of Juno: who (accompanied by Sleep)

    ——— " with gliding ease swam thro' the air
    " To IDA's Mount—at LECTOS first
    " They quitted ocean, overpassing high
    " The dry land, while beneath their feet the woods
    " Their spiry summits wav'd. There, unperceiv'd
    " By Jove, SLEEP mounted IDA's loftiest pine—
    " Then swift to GARGARUS, on IDA's top
    " The Goddess soar'd."———

If it be insisted that the mountain immediately over Troy, is the true *Gargarus*, why should Juno, who came from the quarter of *Lemnos* and *Imbros*, land at *Lectum*, so far out of the way?

[c] Dr. Pocock is an exception. However, until the publication of M. Kauffer's map, (though *a bad copy*,) by Dr. Clarke and Mr. Cripps, the Public had the most incorrect ideas, possible, of *Ida* and the *Troad*.

Ida, the ridge towards Troy; or at least, they exclude *Gargarus*. The former, in describing the march of Xerxes, northward, from *Pergamus, Thebe,* and *Antandros,* to *Ilium,* makes him " leave Ida on his LEFT hand," that is to the WEST. (Polym. 42) Now the summit of *Gargarus* being little short of an English mile, in altitude (775 toises, French), what should have induced Xerxes to lead his army over such a ridge, when he might have gone a straighter and smoother road, by avoiding it; and after all, he must of necessity have crossèd the *western* ridge, also, in order to arrive at Ilium?

Again, Xenophon says, (Anab. vii.) that in his way [southward] from *Ilium,* through *Antandros,* to *Adramyttium,* he *crossed M. Ida.* Of course, it must have been the *western* and *southern* ranges; as is done at present by those who travel from the Dardanelles to Eidermit, or *Adramyttium.*[d]

Strabo unquestionably refers the ideas of Demetrius, respecting the Mountain of *Cotylus* (i. e. *Gargarus*) and its rivers, to the TROJAN IDA; never supposing that the lofty mountain over *Antandros* and *Gargara,* was *Cotylus, the*

[d] Since the above was written, the Author has seen, in the second volume of Dr. Clarke's Travels, Mr. Walpole's route from *Alexandria Troas* to *Adramyttium,* over the *western* and *southern* ridges of *Ida.* He finds also the same route in Le Brun: and in M. Choiseul Gouffier's second volume.

Mr. Walpole's account of this short journey is highly illustrative of the course and nature of the two chains of Ida, which he passed.

The route in Le Brun, which led from Adramyttium to Papazli, Narli, Felampe, Lerissi, and Kemalli, to Koum-kala, appears to be that of the ordinary caravans; and we cannot but believe that Dr. Clarke misconceived the route of the caravan, given in his Vol. II. page 137, where he supposes it to have passed by the *east* of Mount *Gargarus,* or high Ida.

There is another route from Lerissi to Koum-kala, by way of Ene, and Bounarbashi.

highest point of Ida; from whence Demetrius derives the fountains of the *Scamander,* the *Esepus,* and the *Granicus,* (page 602). Strabo concluded that all these rivers sprung from that chain of Ida bordering on the Trojan plain, which he had in view from the sea coast; and which, it appears, was the *only* Ida known to him.[e] Yet he describes the position of the *City of Gargara,* at 260 stadia to the eastward of the *Lectum* Promontory, with the Mountain of *Gargarus* above it: and he had before him, the distance of *Cotylus* from *Scepsis,* and of this latter from *Palæ Scepsis,* in the report of Demetrius.   But it appears clearly that he was not in the habit of subjecting his *written* geography to the test of tabular construction; whence, in some cases, its accuracy and consistency, were never put to the proof.

Conceiving, therefore, that the highest part of the *Trojan* Ida, or of the ridge next to him, was the *Cotylus* of Demetrius, Strabo referred (p. 603) the positions of *Palæ Scepsis, Ænea, Polichna,* and the Silver Mine (all of which were really situated under that part of the Trojan Ida), to *Cotylus.* But *Cotylus* lay 20 or more miles farther to the eastward; and belonged to a different chain of mountains.   He also describes the *Æsepus* River, to be no more than 30 stadia from *Palæ Scepsis* (p. 603); although it is described by Demetrius to flow from *Cotylus,* towards the *Propontis;* or to the opposite quarter from the Troad.

Eski Skupchu, or *Old*[f] Skupchu, was found by Dr. Pocock, and other modern travellers, at the eastern foot of the highest part of the Trojan Ida; seven or eight miles to the eastward of *Alexandria Troas:* and this is universally allowed

---

[e] See the first note to page 7.   [f] *Eski* being the Turkish word for *old.*

to be the *Palæ Scepsis* of Strabo. At a few miles to the northward of it, is also found *Ene,* taken for the *Ænea* of Strabo, given at 50 stadia from the former. Again, a silver mine, said by Strabo to lie between *Palæ Scepsis* and *Polichna* (which two places are said by him, page 603, to be near each other) is also found within two miles of the former. Here then are three points of comparison: and as the village of Balouk-li is also found *near* Eski Skupchu, one may conceive this to be *Polichna,* or *Polikna;* and the agreement between the ancient and modern geography will be still closer. (See the Map of the Troad, N°. VI.; and also M. Kauffer's Map of the same Tract.)

Now, the river mentioned by Strabo, at 30 stadia from *Palæ Scepsis,* could not be the *Æsepus;* which, as we have seen, rises in Kasdagh, or *Gargarus,* and flows to the *eastward,* and into the *Propontis;* but must be the Mender (*Scamander*) which flows *westward* from the same mountain; and really passes at about the aforesaid distance from Eski-Skupchu: or in other words *Palæ Scepsis.* One must therefore suspect that the name *Æsepus* has been *interpolated,* and that *Scamander* stood in the original of Demetrius; but that it was altered, from an idea that the context required it. Strabo indeed says (page 602,) that the *Scamander* rises in the mountains; but he probably thought those mountains belonged to the *Trojan* Ida.

With the above clue, one may trace the error of Strabo, respecting the position of the mountain, which gave rise to the *Æsepus, Scamander,* and *Granicus;* and without which, the useful part of his information, respecting this quarter, would be lost. Therefore, what he says respecting *Ida,* has a reference to the chain of mountains over *Ilium* and *Alex-andria Troas*: and that, respecting *Cotylus* and its rivers, *Carasena*, &c. &c.; to *Gargarus*, and the tract lying to the eastward of it.

Scepsis is said (Strabo, page 607) to be 60 stadia from *Palæ Scepsis*;[g] but no line of direction is given. It may be conceived to lie towards *Cotylus*, or *Gargarus*; as the whole distance between *Palæ Scepsis* and *Cotylus*, is given at 180 stadia: (that is, 60 to *Scepsis*, and 120 thence to *Cotylus*;) whilst the distance on Kauffer's map is $6\frac{2}{3}$ French leagues, or about 20 B. miles, from Eski Skupchu to the *hither foot* of Kasdagh, or *Gargarus*. The 180 stades, if taken for Roman, are equal to about 21 such miles; but if on Strabo's scale (of 700 to 1°.) to 18 only. The difference, in either case, is not so great, as to destroy the probability of Kasdagh and Eski Skupchu being the places intended; since the reports of so many persons, worthy of credit, have established the fact of the distance, and of the circumstances of the ground; as Dr. Pocock, Messrs. Kauffer, Carlyle, Hawkins, Clarke, &c.: all of whom agree, that the Mender flows from Kasdagh (the loftiest summit of Ida, situated over *Adra-myttium*, and the site of *Antandros*; &c.) westward to the Plain of Troy; and to the *Hellespont*.

Homer, when he derives not only the *Scamander*, but the *Æsepus* and *Granicus*, &c. also, from Mount Ida,[h] could only

[g] The Latin translation of Casaubon has, erroneously, *forty* instead of *sixty*.

[h] Iliad, lib. xii. v. 19; (Cowper, v. 23) where he makes the *Æsepus* and *Granicus*, &c. which flow from the *eastern* side of Ida, and into the PROPONTIS, *turn back over the tops of the mountains, that give rise to them*, to assist in the demolition of the Grecian rampart. This appears to be a most extraordinary license, considered even as a poetical one.

intend the eastern ridge. He knew the geography well, and extended the region of Ida from *Zeleia,* near the *Propontis,* to the Promontory of *Lectum,* in *Troas;* and, therefore, it is probable, had remarked the principal features of it, on every side. But it may be also, when he describes the ascent of Juno, that he only spoke to the eye; and as the landscape would have appeared to a spectator in the Trojan Plain; since, viewed from that side, the Promontory of *Lectum* appears to be a continuation of the Trojan Ida, the wide valley that separates it, being shut up, in the perspective.[i]

On the whole, then, it appears, that the *Cotylus* of Demetrius, was the *Gargarus* and *Alexandrea* of Strabo; and that it answers to the Kasdagh of the present time; the highest peak of Ida: and situated opposite to the head of the Gulf of *Adramyttium.* As also, that the Mender flows westward from the same mountain, through the vallies of Ida, into the Trojan Plain; and therefore answers (as will presently be shewn) to the *Scamander* of Demetrius: it being, moreover, joined by the way, by a river from the N E. answering to the *Andrius* of Strabo, from the quarter of *Carasena* : (page 602) And finally, that Herodotus, Xenophon, and Strabo, evidently exclude from their ideas of Ida, the mountain and ridge of *Gargarus:* in which they were followed by the modern travellers, Pocock alone excepted; until the date of the late researches of the French gentlemen, resident at Constantinople.

See Mr. Gell's Views, in his Troy, Nos. IV. V. and more particularly No. XIX from the *Tumulus* of Antilochus. The sharp-peaked mountain in the *nearest* range, seen a little to the right of *Gargarus,* appears to be the *Gargarus* of Captain Francklin, and others who considered the western ridge as the *only* Ida.

E

M. D'Anville was totally mistaken, in his ideas of the geography of Mount Ida, and the courses of the rivers of the *Troad*. And this may serve as a proof of the total misconception that must have prevailed in those times respecting *Ida* and *Troas*: since HE was likely to be the best informed of any one, on such subjects.

He places *Cotylus* nearly in the parallel of Troy; although it be nearer that of the *Lectum* Promontory: and at the distance of only 20 MP. from Troy, although it be 30. But following Demetrius, he derives the *Scamander, Æsepus,* and *Granicus,* from *Cotylus*. However, from the difficulty of believing that the source of the *Scamander* was so far distant from *Scepsis*, as is represented by Demetrius, he places *Cotylus* too near to Troy; and *Scepsis* on the *further*, or *eastern* side of *Cotylus* (*i. e. Gargarus*); thus reversing the order of things, as may be seen by comparing the geography of the Troad, in his Map of Asia Minor, with ours in N° VI. founded on the authority of M. Kauffer, &c. M. D'Anville has also followed Strabo, in supposing that there were no other ridges of Ida, save the one facing Troy. So that he has placed *Scepsis* in respect of Ida *Gargarus,* as it really stood, in respect of the *Trojan* Ida.

Had *Scepsis, Palæ Scepsis, Polichna,* &c. been where M. D'Anville has placed them, they would not have been in *Troas*, as they confessedly ought to be; but in *Carasena*.

But it is however, certain, that by his deriving the *Scamander* from *Cotylus,* he meant to follow the opinion of Demetrius: and that he had no idea of its springing from the Plain, in front of Troy, according to the system of M. de Chevalier.

SECTION III.

A COMPARISON OF THE REPORT OF DEMETRIUS OF SCEPSIS
WITH THE ACTUAL TOPOGRAPHY OF THE TROAD.

Description of the Plain *of* Troy, *by* Demetrius—*It seems to
agree generally with the actual landscape—Aids derived
from* Mr. Gell, *in the application of the above description —
The* Scamander *of Demetrius answers clearly to the* Mender;
and the Andrius River, *its Adjunct, to the* Lidgex *of*
M. Kauffer—*Districts of* Cebrenia *and* Carasena—*their
position—Ridge which divides the* Scamandrian, *from the*
Simoïsian, *Plain, recognized—The Ancients right, in respect
of the general position of* Ancient Troy—*The adoption of
the erroneous System of* M. de Chevalier, *has arrested the
Progress of Enquiry in the proper quarter—Means of recti-
fying his Errors, furnished by* Mr. Gell—*and by* Professor
Carlyle—*The* Shimar River *pointed out by the latter, for-
merly recognised by* Dr. Pocock; *and now by* Dr. Clarke—
Supposed Tumulus *of* Myrinna *or* Batiæa—*Position of* New
Ilium, *from Ancient Documents—The different Courses of
the* Shimar, *in Summer and Winter, accounted for — The*
Shimar, *doubtless the* Simoïs; *as the* Mender *the* Scamander
—*Many ancient Names of Rivers preserved in Asia Minor—
The* Kalli-colone, *or beautiful hill, recognized in the hil o*
Atchekui.—*Bounarbashi Hill, the site of some Ancient City.*

Having given a detailed account of the geography of the
principal members of Ida, which have so close a connexion
with the subject of Troy, we proceed to give the remarks of

Demetrius, on the supposed scene of the Iliad : the general scope of whose information is as follows : (Strabo, p. 597).

" From the tract of [Western] IDA, two *Elbows*, or projecting ridges of the mountain, extend themselves towards the sea ; one in the direction of *Rhoeteum*, the other of *Sigæum* :[k] and bending in a semicircular form, include within them both the *Simoïsian* Plain, through which flows the *Simoïs* : and also the *Scamandrian* Plain, which is, in like manner, watered by the *Scamander* : which latter Plain, is also named the *Trojan*, or *Iliean*."[l]

" The terminations of these mountainous (or hilly) projections, in the plain, are at about the same distance from the sea,[m] as the *present Ilium* ; which is situated *between them*, as the site of the *Ancient Ilium* is between the places of their commencement [near Ida]."

" The Scamandrian Plain is the broadest of the two ; and in it most of the battles, described by the poet, were fought. *In it, we are also shewn* the *Erineus*, the *barrow of Æsyetes*, the *Batiæa*, and the *Monument of Ilus*."

" The rivers *Scamander* and *Simoïs*, the *latter* by directing its course towards *Sigæum*, and the former towards *Rhœteum*, unite their streams, a little in front of the present [i. e. the New] *Ilium* : and the confluent stream discharges itself

[k] See the Map, compartments Nº. I. and II.

[l] When the Grecian army was first marshalled at the ships, and marched towards the Plain of Troy, it was said (lib. ii. v. 465. Cowper, v. 526), that they were in the *Scamandrian Plain*. This was, of course, below *both* of the confluences ; and Homer no where speaks of a *Simoïsian* Plain, as distinct from the *Scamandrian*. It is Demetrius alone, who distinguishes the Plains.

[m] By the *Sea*, the *Ægean* only can be intended.

towards *Sigæum :* forming first the *Stoma-limne,* or *Lake of the Mouth.*"

" Finally, a narrow ridge divides each of the above Plains from the other; beginning near the present Ilium, and reaching as far as *Cebrenia ;* forming the shape of the letter Υ towards the above hilly projections, as it joins to either side."[n]

" The village of the Ilieans, where ANCIENT ILIUM, or TROY, *is supposed to have stood,* is 30 stadia from the present Ilium." (In page 593, it is said " *towards the East, and Ida.*") " And beyond *that,* at 10 stadia, is the *Kalli-colone; near which the Simoïs flows, at the distance of five stadia.*" [Strabo, page 597].

This description (as far as it can be understood, by comparing it with the actual topography) seems to be allowed to be just, even by M. de Chevalier, and by those who have adopted his system; the application of the names of the rivers excepted.[o]

The projecting ridges from Ida, described by Demetrius, which envelope the scene of the Iliad, are easily understood to mean those two ranges, between which the Mender and its branches flow, in their course to the *Hellespont :* the range on the south detaching itself from that part of Western Ida, over Bounarbashi, and terminating at Erkessi-kui ; and that from the north, which, separating the Valley of Thymbrek (*Thymbra*) from the coast of the *Hellespont ;* has its termination at the promontory, on which the tumulus of

[n] This cannot well be understood, for want of a more detailed, and *more accurate topography* of the hilly tract towards Ida.

[o] See again in the Map, compartments N°. I. IV. and VI.

In Tepé, (or of Ajax) stands : anciently *Rhoeteum.* It will appear, by Mr. Gell's distinct and beautiful view, N°. XIX. (from the *Tumulus* ascribed to Antilochus) that the general appearance of the landscape, justifies the description given by Demetrius : nor is there any other spot near the *Helles-pont,* that resembles it, in any degree.

With respect to the distinct course of each of the *two* rivers, previous to their junction near *New Ilium,* the descrip-tion agrees well with the supposition, that the Shimar was the *Simoïs,* and the Mender, the *Scamander.* For, it is natu-rally understood that, previous to their intercepting each others course, the river which pointed towards *Sigæum,* must have been the eastern one, or that to the *right,* which would answer to the *Shimar :* and the one which pointed towards *Rhoeteum,* the western, or left hand river; which agrees to the *Mender.*[p] It may indeed be said, that the same result might have been produced by the Mender and Bounarbashi rivers; the former considered as the *Simoïs,* and the latter, as the *Scamander :* but it does not appear so probable that the Bounarbashi River ever ran near New Ilium, as that the Mender did.

Much more conclusive, however, respecting the identity of the *Scamander,* is the testimony of Demetrius concerning the source of that river, in the distant mountains near *An-tandros* (Strabo, page 602); and its western course from thence to the Troad; since, in that course, it is said to sepa-rate the country of *Cebrenia* from that of *Scepsis :* a circum-stance that can apply only to the Mender; which really

---

[p] M. de Chevalier translates Strabo differently; conducting the *Scamande* towards *Sigæum,* the *Simoïs* towards *Rhoeteum.* (Eng. Transl. p. 63.)

takes a westerly course, between countries which alone can be taken for *Cebrenia* and *Scepsis*.[q] This circumstance therefore, appears decisive of its being the *Scamander*, intended by Demetrius.

It is also said by Strabo, page 602 (and doubtless on the same authority of Demetrius) that the river *Andrius*, from the quarter of *Carasena*, joins the *Scamander*. *Carasena* was a country that bordered on *Dardania*, and extended to *Zeleia*: consequently, the *Andrius* answers to the *Lidgex* of Kauffer's map; which joins the Mender, in the heart of Ida, and has most of its sources from the mountains adjacent to *Carasena*: that is the chain of eastern Ida, or *Gargarus*. (See Kauffer's Map of the Troad: and N°. VI. of the Map belonging to this Tract, which is founded on it.)

It may also be remarked, that the river of Bounarbashi, the *Scamander* of M. de Chevalier, *has no adjunct stream whatsoever*: nor could it receive any from the quarter of *Carasena*, because the Mender interposes. Consequently, the Bounarbashi River *cannot*, consistently with this account, have been the *Scamander* of Demetrius. And this particular, the reader is requested to bear in mind.

It also appears, that the *Scamandrian* and *Simoïsian* plains of Demetrius, were separated from each other by a ridge of elevated land, or low hills, which commenced near the modern Ilium, and extended upwards (eastwards) to *Cebrenia*: that is, to the foot of the *Trojan* Ida; and to the two hilly ridges that embraced the *Troad*. But no *high land*

[q] For *Cebrenia* bordered on Ancient Troy; and by the context, (Strabo, page 597) lay to the eastward of it: *Scepsis* to the south, and south east. See again, N°. VI.

is found within the tract, between the Mender and Bounarbashi Rivers : the Trojan Plain of M. Chevalier.[r] Such,
however, *is found*, on the opposite, or eastern side of the
Mender, and between that river and another to the northward of it, named *Shimar*, by some ; by others, *Simores*.

As this river presents quite a new feature in the *recent*
Topography of the Troad (though not, it seems, unknown, in
earlier times) it will be necessary to introduce it, with considerable detail, to the notice of the reader.

Previous to the promulgation of the new system of M. de
Chevalier, the Moderns (as the Ancients had done), sought
the site of TROY, on the *east*, or *Idæan* side of the Mender ;
concluding that the Shimar, or Simores (the next river in
that direction) as well probably from the name, as from the
relative situation, was the *Simoïs* of antiquity.   Sandys,
Pocock, and Lady M. W. Montagu, all speak to this effect ;
and M. D'Anville adopted much the same idea.   But M.
Chevalier has turned the attention of travellers, almost ex-
clusively, to the opposite, or *Ægean* side of the Mender : so
that the progress of enquiry, on the *Idæan* side, where Demetrius believed Troy to have stood, has been completely
arrested : each traveller appearing to vie with the other, in
giving authority to M. de Chevalier's system ; trusting impli-
citly to his topography, in despite of their own observations
(Mr. Gell excepted), although M. de Chevalier had converted
a *wide plain* into a *hilly region ;* and placed Troy on hills,

---

[r] M. de Chevalier, in quoting the description of the Trojan Plain, &c. from
Demetrius, *stops short* at the *ridge of high land*, described above in page 29.
(See his description of the Plain of Troy, Eng. Transl. p. 62.)

although the poet had declared that it was situated in a plain.

And here it becomes necessary to repeat, (howsoever unpleasant the task) that the inaccuracies of M. de Chevalier's Map of the Plain of Troy, are so gross, as totally to mislead the judgment of his readers; *and to preclude the possibility of judging aright.* For the map leaves only a *mere slip* of plain, on the east of the Mender; although Mr. Gell shews us, as well in his plan, as in the text of his book, that this Plain is by far the widest of the two. And on the other hand, M. de Chevalier has represented the Plain between the Bounarbashi and Mender, *out of all proportion*, the widest: and this is HIS Plain of Troy.

Again, he has *totally omitted* the river *Shimar* and its valley; and substituted for them, those of Thymbrek: whilst the places of the latter, are occupied by a hilly tract. Never, perhaps, did a series of errors so effectually combine to exclude truth. For who would look for a plain, in a place where no plain was represented to exist; or for the *Simoïs* in the Vale of *Thymbra?*

The plan of the Plain of Troy, by Mr. Gell (N°. XLV.), together with his View from the Tumulus of Antilochus (N°. XIX.) will sufficiently prove the truth of this remark. Besides which, he gives, in the text of his book, the clearest proofs of it, as may be seen by an extract in the note, at the foot of the page.[t] These remarks most fully prove the great

---

[s] See a reduced copy of it, N°. III. The reader is requested to compare it with M. Kauffer's on the *right*, and Mr. Gell's on the *left*.

[t] " A line drawn from Kalifatli to Koum-*kui* (it may be suspected that Koum-*kala* is intended, as the remark agrees only with that place) would leave the

extent of the plain on the *east* of the Mender, where M. de Chevalier does not admit the existence of *any* plain, between the mouth of the Thymbrek Valley and Atchekui: and it will be found that the several views, taken from different points by Mr. Gell, are in harmony with his Plans and Remarks.

Professor Carlyle, in 1800, traversed the ground of the Troad, and its adjacencies, in various directions (See N°. V). He visited Ene (*Ænia*) and the Springs of the Mender; and ascended Kas-dagh (the *Cotylus* of Demetrius), the highest point of Ida; from whence the Mender flows. (See N°. VI.) But, more to the present purpose, he went from Jenishehr (*Sigæum*) to In-Tepe, the Tumulus of Ajax, and thence to Koum-kui (See again N°. V.) From this place, he ascended the Valley of Thymbrek, to the village of that name; and from thence traced a most important line, to Bounarbashi; intersecting the upper course of the Shimar River; the position of Atchekui (the supposed *Kalli-colone* of the Iliad); and the course of the Mender: thus supplying, in some

hill of *Ilium Recens*, more than a mile to the east." (See A B in N°. I.) Again, " A line drawn from the mouth of the river, to the *Tumuli* above Bounarbashi, passes through the western point of the hill, where Kauffer places the City of Constantine; [though in reality, it was *New Ilium*] between which and the Mender is a *wide* plain." (See C D in the same N°. I.) " And lastly, the range of hills on which Chiblak is situated,* does not, in any part, project so far to the south, as to interfere with a right line drawn from the Tomb of Antilochus to Atche-kui." See E F. (Gell's Troy, page 113.) Koum-*kala* and Koum-kui have already been distinguished.

---

* Mr. Gell was not aware of the existence of the Valley of the Shimar; and therefore supposed the whole to be one mass of hills.

measure, what is wanting in Mr. Gell's Map of the Troad.
And finally, he traced another line from Koum-kui, to Bounarbashi, *direct*; intersecting the *winter course* of the Shimar.

From these interesting and useful routes, we learn that a
Torrent River, under the name of *Shimar*, descends from the
western front of Ida, and flows through a valley of its own,
between the courses of the Thymbrek and Mender rivers;
and nearly equidistant from both; and passing near to, and
on the south side of Chiblak, enters the *great Plain* opposite
to Kalifatli, through the opening of the valley seen in
Mr. Gell's view, from the Tomb of Antilochus, (N°. XIX).
Thence, according to Mr. Carlyle, it has *two distinct*, and
widely diverging beds: the one during spring, and in ordinary seasons, when *low* in its bed, along the foot of the hill,
of *New Ilium;* and thence, by Koum-kui, to a junction with
the Mender, not far above the bridge of Koum-kala:[u] pre-
serving its name of Shimar, the whole way.[x]   But during
the season of its swelling, (in winter) it makes a pretty direct
course to the Mender, at, or very near, Kalifatli.

It would appear, that neither Mr. Gell, nor M. Kauffer,
knew, that the water-course which joins the Mender, at

[u] It appears to separate, near the Bridge, into two branches; one of which
joins the Mender, the other gains the sea, by a separate channel. For one branch
was crossed by Mr. Carlyle *between* the *Bridge* and *In Tepe:* the other is
crossed in the ordinary road, between the Bridge and Kalifatli.

[x] Mr. Carlyle remarks that " after the junction of the *Shimar*, with the
" Thymbrek River, the *larger stream* of the Shimar, communicates its name to
" the confluent waters."

We learn from Strabo (page 598) that the *Thymbrius* River joined the
Scamander; which latter, probably, at that time, ran under the site of *Koum-
kui:* as the conflux of the *Scamander* and *Simoïs* was then near *New Ilium.*

Kalifatli, and which they also mark at Chiblak; (that is, the Shimar in question) was traceable any higher up; they considering it as originating at the latter place.

Captain Francklin, in company with Mr. Philip Hope, went nearly over the same ground with Mr. Carlyle, only that they deviated to the *south-east*, between Thymbrek-kui, and Atchekui; and getting entangled amongst the roots of Mount Ida, could not describe the line of their route, so exactly as could be wished.[y] No stream, or torrent-bed, is marked on their map, between the Thymbrek and Mender rivers: but Captain F. says (page 29 of his Tour), that, " during our tour of two days, from entering the *Kalli-colone*, " or chain of hills that constitute Mount Ida, until we " passed Troy [meaning Bounarbashi] to the south-west, " we found among the hills, the beds of *several torrents*."—

In pages 9, 10, and 12, of the same Tour, the *Kalli-colone* is explained to mean the *hilly tract* that commences on the south of the Valley of Thymbrek, and extends to the River Mender: and not the *single Hill* of Atchekui. (See No. I. of the Map.) Of course, the Shimar must be understood to be included among those " *several torrents;*" as Capt. F. must of necessity have crossed it.

It is proper to observe, that Mr. Carlyle traced the Shimar, from the place where he intersected its course, at Eski, (or *Old*), Atchekui, to the foot of the western, or *Trojan* Ida;

---

[y] They ascended the Valley of Thymbrek, one mile beyond Thymbrek-kui, to the ruins of a *Doric* temple, at a place named *Thymbrek Muzarlik;* or the Cemetery of Thymbrek. They had previously visited the greater temple at Kalil-Eli; which Captain Francklin describes to have been of the *Corinthian* order; pages 8, and 9. More will be said respecting the position of the former temple.

2¾ miles, in an E. b. S. direction. And at that place he found an aqueduct, that was built across it. Concerning this aqueduct, no particulars are known to the author.

Lady Mary Wortley Montagu, in 1718, viewed the courses and confluence of the Mender and Shimar. She names the latter of these rivers, Simores. Sandys (1610) does the same. He says, " Twixt these two capes, there lieth a spacious " valley. Nearer *Sigæum* was the station for the Grecian " navy : but nearer *Rhæteum*, the River *Simoïs*, (NOW CALLED " SIMORES) dischargeth itself into the *Hellespont* —Two, not " far disjoining vallies there are, that stretch to each other, " and join in an ample plain.—Through *these vallies*, glide " *Simoïs* and divine *Scamander.*"

Both of these persons viewed the rivers from Jenishehr (*Sigæum*): and as the River of Bounarbashi, it may be concluded, had long before ceased to flow into the Mender, this latter river, together with the Shimar, must have been the two rivers intended. The vallies, " joining in an ample plain," must be supposed to be those of Thymbrek, and of the Mender : it being probable that Sandys concluded, that the Shimar, from the direction of the lower part of its course, came through the Valley of Thymbrek, which presented a wider opening than that of the Shimar; or Chiblak. (See N°. I. of the Map.)

We have been thus particular, here, in order to shew that the name *Shimar*, or *Simores*, so much alike in root to *Simoïs*, still keeps its ground in the Troad.

Most of the late travellers have continued the name of Thymbrek, (or Dumbrek) to the stream that descends through the Valley of that name; *after* it has received the Shimar; and even to its junction with the Mender. Mr. Carlyle seems to be the only one, who, in our times, has made the distinction. (See note to page 35.) The rest might easily take it for granted, that the same name of Thymbrek was continued.

Dr. Pocock[z] traced the course of the Mender (which he calls the *Scamander*), downwards from Ene: then crossed the *high land* between the Mender, and the river, which he calls the *Simoïs*, not far above the *conflux:* and finally, the Thymbrek River, in his way to *Abydus.* It must be concluded, that his route certainly lay through Chiblak, Kalil-Eli,[a] and Erinkui: therefore, the conflux alluded to should be that at Kalifatli; which lay from $2\frac{1}{2}$ to 3 miles on the left: that is, the west.

It may be remarked, that he calls the second river, the *Simoïs:* whether he meant to apply the supposed ancient name, as he had done before, that of *Scamander*, to the Mender; or that the name Shimar, or Simores, appeared so much like *Simoïs*, that he applied it accordingly.

These, although very general notices, yet from so honest and unbiassed a man as Dr. Pocock, are perfectly convincing, in respect of the *existence* of such a river as the Shimar; even had no other authority been adduced.

It was his idea that TROY had been situated on the *high land* just mentioned, between Bounarbashi and Chiblak:[b]

---

[z] Vol. II. part 2d, page 108.   [a] Or Halil-Eli.

[b] That is, of course, the *Pergama,* or Citadel: for the city itself stood either in the Plain, or on an easy slope. It is probable that Dr. Pocock actually passed over a part of its site, in the Plain.

REPORT OF DEMETRIUS OF SCEPSIS.

REPORT OF DEMETRIUS OF SCEPSIS.

following, probably, the ideas of Demetrius and Strabo, amongst the ancients, and those of most of the modern travellers, down to his own time.

Dr. Chandler saw the winter conflux, near Kalifatli; but unaccountably calls the Shimar, or Kalifatli River, the *Scamander*; and the Mender, the *Simoïs*; in the Map prefixed to his Travels in Asia Minor.

Dr. Murdoch Mackenzie (in May 1742) describes the river that passes by Koum-kui, and thence to the Mender, near the bridge of Koum-kala, under the name of Dumbrek. (Thymbrek): and says, that " it is thought to be the *Simoïs*." The river, he says, was " pretty deep; but rather a standing " than a running water : full of grass and mud." It must be recollected that the *Simoïs*, like the *Scamander*, was no more than a *torrent;* but Dr. Mackenzie speaks of the lower part of its course, through the *Alluvial Soil.*[d]

The ridge of elevated land between the Mender and Shimar Rivers, is described in Mr. Gell's Plan, N°. XLV. and certainly has an agreement with the Report of Demetrius.[e]   Dr. Chandler, who was on the spot, says, that about

[c] From MSS. in the possession of my friend, R. H. Inglis, Esq.

[d] Dr. Clarke has added the most complete testimony respecting the existence of this river, which he *names* from the village of *Kalifatli ;* but considers it as the *Simoïs*. (Vol. 2, page 96.)   His description is, that of a *torrent.*   At the time he saw it, (March,) it was stagnant; forming deep holes, so as to be fordable only in particular places.   He reckons it *not less* than the Bounarbashi River ; but it is surely much larger : He perhaps spoke of the Volume of Water, *then* in it.   It may be remarked, that as Dr. Clarke traced its course, where it takes the form of a *torrent ;* so Dr. Mackenzie traced it through its *alluvions* lower down ; and where its course was sluggish.

[e] See above, page 29.

Kalifatli, there is a *swell of ground* that prevents a view of the *upper Plain* of the *Scamander*, from Jenishehr: for until he had advanced to Kalifatli, he was ignorant of the existence of any such Plain.[f] This swell appears to be a projection from the just mentioned ridge of elevated land.

Doctor Clarke communicated to Mr. Gell, his discovery of a Tumulus, in the Plain above Kalifatli: and which Mr. Gell supposes (we conceive with reason) to be that of *Myrinna*, or *Batiœa*. The description added, " that it was " connected with a rising ground of easy ascent; and insu- " lated with regard to other eminences in the vicinity." (Troy, pages 56, and 117.) This *rising ground* is probably the *swell* noticed by Dr. Chandler.[g]

Doctor Chandler also saw, when near Kalifatli, two *Tumuli* in the Plain to the eastward; and a third on a brow to his left. He reports that he saw in his front, a little to the right of east, the channel of the Mender. Another river joined it in the Plain; and which he did not find in Mr. Wood's Map.—Before him, across the channel, and a little to the right, he saw the distant tops of two tall barrows, covered with green turf: and *behind them*, towards Mount Ida, was the large, conical, well formed hill, which he called *Kalli-colone*. Again, on his *left*, on the edge of the Plain, and on a brow, was a very conspicuous Barrow.[h]

---

[f] From a MS. obligingly communicated by a friend.

[g] Dr. Clarke also noticed a swell of ground, or lengthened mound; but this he describes to be situated on the *north* side of the Kalifatli River; for after tracing the mound, and observing two *tumuli* near it, he crossed the Kalifatli River, and then traced its *southern* bank, to Kalifatli Village. (See Vol. II. p. 93, *et seq.*

[h] This seems to have been the one named by M. Kauffer the Tumulus of Ilus.

Of the two *Tumuli* in the Plain, the Doctor regarded the nearest, and that to the *left*, as the Monument of *Ilus;* the most distant, and to the *right*, as that of *Myrinna*, or *Batiæa*. As they were seen in the line between Kalifatli, and the conical hill, (doubtless Atchekui), one of them, and probably that to the right, may well be taken for the *Tumulus*, pointed out by Doctor Clarke: and although no just idea of their distance, from Doctor Chandler's station, can be collected, yet from the circumstances of the description, they were probably not far off.

The place of conflux of the two rivers, in the time of Demetrius, is easily *approximated*, since it is given in a general way, in respect of *New Ilium*, a known position in the present geography. For as it is said that the conflux was a little in *front of* New Ilium, one may conclude that it was at no great distance from it; and probably within a mile.[i]

New Ilium is thus placed. In the Antonine Itinerary it is given at 12 Roman miles from *Dardanus*, which was itself 9 from *Abydus*. total 21 MP. equal to 15 G. miles in direct distance from *Abydus*. And from *Alexandria Troas*, it was 16 M P; both in the Itinerary, and in the Theodosian Tables; and these are equal to $11\frac{1}{2}$ G. miles, direct. And finally, it was 12 stadia from the nearest part of the sea coast, (that is, the bay formed by the Promontories of *Sigæum* and *Rhæteum*), in the time of Demetrius.

The total distance between *Abydus* and *A. Troas*, is therefore given at 37 MP; equal to $26\frac{1}{2}$ G. miles direct: and on

[i] See above, page 28.

the construction, 25½ are measured; so that the difference is small. And the 16 from *Alexandria Troas*, or 11½ G. miles; agreeing with the position of the hill, at about a mile to the S. E. of Koum-kui, where there are great ruins; and also inscriptions,[k] which are said to identify them, as being those of *New Ilium;* no doubt can remain. And with respect to its distance from the coast, which is now nearly two miles, the difference between that and the 12 stadia, may well be accounted for, by accretion, in the course of nearly 2000 years. In effect, there is no other position that suits it: and that it was on a *hill*, or elevated ground, we learn from Strabo, page 599.[l]

The place of conflux, then, in the time of Demetrius, was *near* New Ilium; but in what direction it lay, is not mentioned: however, be it where it might, it affords a proof that the Scamander, in ancient times, ran on the side of *Rhœteum;* otherwise it could not have *approached* New Ilium.

It has appeared, in page 35, that, at the present day, the

[k] See Mr. Gell's Troy, page 117.

[l] Dr. Clarke (Vol. II. p. 102) visited the ruins of a magnificent city, named by the people of the neighbourhood, *Old Kalifatli;* and which are undoubtedly those of the *New Ilium.* But we are unable to trace him on the Map; and consequently to fix on the spot; which is greatly to be regretted. He says that it was at a short distance to the eastward of Kalifatli. New Ilium, in Kauffer's Map, is about 1¼; in Gell's about 1½ mile, to the NE of Kalifatli: and therefore, has a general agreement with the report. But the Doctor's Map places it 3 miles to the N. E. of Kalifatli.

Shimar, at different seasons, joins the Mender, at different points of its course. Whether this was the case, anciently, cannot now be known: but by the progress of Achilles during the pursuit, after the *last* battle; as well as by the circumstance of the goddesses' alighting at the conflux, to view the *first* battle, fought near the Tomb of Myrinna, (which was itself not far from the *Scæan* Gate of Troy), one must suppose the conflux to have been at that time, much higher up than the site of New Ilium.

The cause which produced the double course, might not then have existed: that is, the raising of the level to a sufficient height, by alluvions. To make this understood, it is necessary to repeat, that the conflux at Kalifatli, according to Mr. Carlyle, exists only during the seasons of floods in the Shimar: and when its bed is filled: for then, as is known by experience, from other rivers of the like kind, it may have elevation, bulk, and force enough, to make its way *direct*, through a bed, partly choaked up by sands; but which in its low and weak state, it has neither weight nor velocity enough to remove: and is therefore compelled to seek a *lower level*, through a more circuitous track. More will be said on this subject hereafter.

The name SHIMAR or SIMORES, as is said above, has doubtless a similitude, in point of *root*, with SIMOÏS: and when coupled with that of its adjunct stream, of the name of MENDER, seemingly the remains of SCAMANDER; who but must *suspect*, from the names alone, that these are the streams immortalized by Homer? And more especially, as there are found, in the same region, so many other modern names of rivers, that agree so nearly with the ancient ones;

as, Meinder for *Mæander;* Sackariah, for *Sangarius* and
Sagarius; Tarsia, for *Tarsius;* Bartin, or Partin, for *Parthe-
nius;* Falios, for *Billæus;* &c. &c. And as Demetrius and
Strabo call the Rivers of the Troad by their *Homeric* names,
without adding any others in explanation, one is warranted
in supposing that they had preserved their ancient names,
to that day, from the date of Homer, and the Trojan War:
and if so, they must be regarded as completely identified, to
the times of Demetrius and of Strabo.

It will be found in the sequel, that the descriptions and
characters of these rivers, as given by Homer, go equally
to prove their identity.[m]

We conceive, then, that the description, both of the
Rivers, Plain, and intermediate ridge of high land, by Demetrius, is made out, in our Topography: and that, after
the above exposition, one can hardly doubt which TWO of
the rivers; and consequently, WHICH of the included tracts
between them, Demetrius meant to describe, as the scene of
the Iliad.   In forming his opinion, he had advantages superior to those which any one of our modern travellers could

---

[m] M. D'Anville (in an enlarged Map of the Troad inserted) in his *Asia
Minor,* has both the Shimar and Thymbrek Rivers, as well as the Mender:
which latter, he justly considers as the *Scamander.* But he takes the river which
occupies the place of the *Thymbrius,* for the *Simoïs; & vice versa.* He probably had found out that the lower part of the Thymbrek was named Shimar, or
Simores; and did not conceive that it was a continuation of the *intermediate*
river, Shimar, joined with the Thymbrek. But how could this system be reconciled to the history of the warfare, at the ships; when a part of the Trojan army
occupied the Valley of *Thymbra, and extended its flank to the sea?*

possess. He was a native, and resident almost on the very spot. His history proves him to have been enthusiastically fond of Homer's writings; and he had leisure to pursue his enquiries. And it cannot be doubted, that various kinds of notices, respecting the subject, must have perished.

In respect of the site of TROY itself, it has appeared (page 29), that he does not absolutely venture to place it; but only says that it was *supposed* to have been at the place where *then* stood the *Pagus Iliensium*, or Village of the Ilieans, 30 stadia from New Ilium, to the eastward; and towards *Ida;* (Strabo, pages 593, 596, and 597); and between the places of commencement of the two ranges of hills, which inclose the Plain of Troy: as New Ilium did, between their termination, near the sea. As the subject will be fully considered in a separate Section, we shall only add, in this place, that Mr. Gell's View, N°. XXXIII. shews a hill in that position, which answers to the *Pagus Iliensium;* and which, in appearance, is suited to the idea given of the *Pergama.*

The *Kalli-colone*, or *beautiful hill*, is said by Demetrius, (See above, page 29), to be ten stadia from the Village of the *Ilieans*, forty from New Ilium.[n] Accordingly, the hill of Atchekui will be found to agree, as well in respect of distance from *New Ilium*, as in its general description: but there is

---

[n] Strabo (page 598, from Demetrius) places the Kalli-colone 40 stadia from New Ilium: and in the preceding page, the same hill is said to be 10 stadia from the *Pagus Iliensium;* and this latter, 30 from New Ilium. Of course, the *Pagus* should have lain in the *direct line* between N. Ilium and the *Kalli-colone*. And, in page 593, this line of direction is said to be *eastward*, and *towards Ida.*

a point of agreement wanting in relative position ; which is, that it is not so near the *Simoïs*, as Homer and Demetrius represent it, if Mr. Carlyle's report of the upper course of the Shimar be correct. It is said, that Mars " fiercely excited the " Trojans; standing, at one time, on *the top of the City ;* " and at another, running *by*, or *near* the *Simoïs*, upon *Kalli-* " *colone.*"° And Strabo, p. 597, " Ten stades above the " *Pagus Iliensium*, is a certain hill named *Kalli-colone; by* " or *near* to which the *Simoïs* flows, at the distance of five " stades."

Now, according to Mr. Carlyle's description of the course of the Shimar River, which is from E. b. S. to W. b. N. from the skirts of Ida, to the place where he crossed it, near *Old* Atchekui ; the hill in question should be a full mile from any part of the Shimar.ᴾ

We state this difficulty, without knowing how to remove it. But it may possibly be, that the course of the Shimar, from the place where Mr. Carlyle crossed it, and thence traced it, upwards to the Aqueduct, (See above, page 36) may be *more northerly* than he supposed ; and even so much, as to bring the Hill of Atchekui, within the distance assigned to the *Kalli-colone*, from the *Simoïs*.

The rest of the description is satisfactory. Many persons who have viewed it, have been struck with its appearance ; it being completely insulated, and of the form of a flatted hay-cock. But it more particularly forces itself on the view

° Iliad, lib. xx. v. 51.

ᴾ It may be remarked, however, that it is *still farther* from the River *Mender*, the *Simoïs* of M. de Chevalier.

from the lower part of the Plain.q Therefore, the imagination of Homer, no doubt, on 'his first view of the scene, seized on it, to seat the Gods of Troy on: it being moreover, at the upper extremity of the Plain, and on a *rise;* whilst the rampart of the Greeks, on which Minerva sat, was at its lower extremity. According to the perspective views of it, in Mr. Gell's Troy, it may not unaptly be compared to our *Primrose Hill.*r

And here it may be remarked, that surely Homer meant to place the *Kalli-colone* within the same Plain, in which Troy itself was situated; and in which the battles were fought. But M. Chevalier assigns them different Plains! But, in truth, the person who would wish to be set right, should avoid all reference to M. Chevalier's statements, and consult those of M. Kauffer and Mr. Gell: the latter more particularly, as he enters much more into detail, of the part referred to, in N°. XLV. And in addition to this, he ought to consult the same Gentleman's views of the landscape from the different points; which, compared with the plan, will put him in complete possession of the ground.

There is little doubt, that there was either a city, or fortress, or both, on the hill above Bounarbashi; but Demetrius could not but have known all that the different European

q Dr. Chandler, who viewed it from Kalifatli, says, " a large, conical, well-formed hill, which I called *Kalli-colone.* (MSS.)

See the Views N°. xix. xxviii. xxix. xxxiii. and xxxvi.; but particularly xix. and xxxiii. from different quarters.

The name of this hill and village is spelt differently: Professor Carlyle has *Akshi-kui:* M. Kauffer and others *Aktché;* Mr. Gell and M. de Chevalier, *Atche;* and Captain Francklin *Atch.*

travellers know, concerning the remains of cities in the Troad. In like manner, surely, the *springs* at Bounarbashi must have been familiar to him, as to every other person in that quarter: and yet HE could find no springs that answered to those spoken of by Homer.

PART II.

———

A COMPARISON OF THE TOPOGRAPHY OF TROY, &c. AS DE-
SCRIBED BY HOMER, WITH THAT GIVEN BY DEMETRIUS;
AND WITH THE ACTUAL TOPOGRAPHY.

PART II

PART II.

SECTION 1.

COMPARISON OF THE TOPOGRAPHY AS DESCRIBED BY
HOMER, WITH THAT BY DEMETRIUS; AND WITH THE
ACTUAL TOPOGRAPHY.

Homer appears to have studied the Scene of the Iliad—His
Scamander agrees in Character and Description with the
Mender: and totally disagrees with the Bounarbashi River
—Proofs adduced, from the Iliad—The Simoïs less discrimi-
nated—Achilles when in pursuit of the Trojans, crosses the
Scamander below the conflux — General Agreement of
Homer's Description of the Plain of Troy, with that between
the Mender and Shimar—The two Springs pointed out by
M. de Chevalier, as the hot and cold Spring of Homer,
proved to be both of the same temperature—The delusion
attempted to be accounted for—Their appearance, altogether
imposing—General Remarks.

THE accuracy of Homer's Topography, in the *Iliad*, has
been a theme of praise at all times. He would, of course,
avoid topographical *details*, as being neither necessary, nor
convenient: nor suited to the dignity of his Poem. It was,
however, necessary, that a field should be marked out; and
also set with objects, as points of rest, to assist the imagination. The boundaries of that field were rivers, which

were themselves to act a part in the drama. IDA, bearing
the throne of Jupiter; with the city of Troy, and the *Kalli-
colone*, beneath it; terminated, in the perspective, the upper
end of the field : the two Promontories, the Port and Camp
of the Greeks, with Neptune, the lower end. The Tombs of
Myrinna and of *Ilus*, are points on which he occasionally
marshals the armies at either end : whilst certain intermediate objects, as the fords, the confluence, and the Erineus,
mark the advance or retreat of the contending armies. The
Tomb of *Æsyetes* is a point to reconnoitre from ; the Vale of
Thymbra, a military station. This description may probably
be considered as addressed to people who knew the ground,
and the objects within it, generally. And considering how
many points of accordance there are, of the ground itself,
with the descriptions in the Poem ; one is warranted in believing that the Poet himself had traversed the field of his
intended Poem : had marked the courses and confluence of
the Rivers; the *Tumuli;* the Bay and Promontories; together with the bearing of the commanding ridge of IDA, and
the HELLESPONT; on the whole scene. Probably too, he
ascended Ida, and warmed his imagination with a view of
the entire landscape, from *Lectos* to *Dardania;* the whole
bordered by the Ægean and Hellespont; and terminated by
the distant lands of *Lesbos, Tenedos, Samo-thrace,* and *Mount
Athos !* [s]

---

[s] The following observations occur in the learned M. HEYNE's Remarks, on
M. de Chevalier's Plain of Troy. (Edinburgh Trans. Vol. IV. p. 78, & 79,
Lit. Class).

" The Poet cannot be read with pleasure, without a sensible representation of
" the face of the country."—" The main circumstance here, is the *general*

Although there are, as we have seen, in and about the Plain of Troy, FOUR rivers, which, at some former period, have collectively formed one *trunk* stream, under the name of *Scamander* (now Mender;)[t] yet it was not required, that the Poet should speak of any more than the TWO adjacent ones, which included the scene of action. If he is silent respecting the River of Bounarbashi, he is equally so with respect to the Thymbrek, or *Thymbrius:* the Valley alone being mentioned, as bearing on the action of the Poem.[u]

As he speaks of no natural eminences in the Plain between his two rivers, save the *Pergama* of Troy, the *Kalli-colone* (or beautiful hill) and the *Erineus* (for the *Throsmos* can only be regarded, as the *ascent* from the Beach), one would be left to conclude, from him, that the remainder of the space, from the bank of one river, to that of the other, was an even Plain. If however, it be admitted, that Homer's Plain

---

" *chart* of the face of the country ; and an establishment of *certain principal*
" *spots.*"

And DR. JOHNSON in his Rasselas :

" The business of a Poet is to remark general properties and large appear-
" ances :—he is to exhibit, in his portraits of nature, such prominent and
" striking features, as recal the original to every mind ; and must neglect the
" minuter discriminations which one may have remarked, and another have
" neglected, for those characteristics, which are alike obvious to vigilance and
" carelessness."

It may be remarked, that in the department of geography, Homer could not venture to indulge his fancy ; as being subject to detection, from the most ordinary class of critics.

[t] When the Bounarbashi joined the Mender, there were four.

[u] The *Thymbrius* River, and *that,* represented by the Bounarbashi, are not mentioned amongst the rivers of Ida, in lib. vii. : the *Scamander* and *Smoïs* alone are mentioned on the Trojan side of Ida.

of Troy, is the same with that of Demetrius, his silence must be accounted for, on this head (if indeed it was at all necessary for him to speak of the ridge of high land that intersects it), because it was unfit for chariots to act on; or, in other words, considering how the contending armies were appointed, unfit for the armies at large to act on.

But, in effect, if the *Tumulus* pointed out by Mr. Gell, for that of *Myrinna,* or *Batiæa,* be really such (and nothing appears to the contrary), the high land does not reach low enough down, to affect the operations of the armies; as they never appear in the Poem to have been higher up than *Myrinna.* For the *swell of ground* spoken of by Dr. Chandler and Mr. Gell, seems to be too gentle in its acclivities, to occasion any impediment to the motion of armies, whether ancient or modern.

Homer's two rivers, *Scamander* and *Simoïs,* cannot be so well identified with those of Demetrius,[x] as with the Mender and Shimar of the present day: and by their *characters and descriptions,* in opposition to those of the River of Bounarbashi; but even their names Mender and Shimar, combined with their *juxta-position,* must be allowed to have some weight in the argument.

But, unaccountably, the advocates for M. de Chevalier's system, have (in our conception) applied the characters of these rivers, perversely. Can it be doubted, in the first instance, that the *Scamander* is intended for the largest of Homer's two rivers? It is occasionally a *furious mountain torrent,* bearing all before it; at other times, a scanty stream, deeply seated, and such as would be diffused over the bottom

[x] See above, page 28, *et seq.*

of a wide channel. And such is the description of the River Mender; whose *bed* is said to be 300 feet wide, and very deep.[y] But the River of Bounarbashi, the *Scamander* of M. de Chevalier, (is fed by regular springs from the edge of the Plain; and has no adjunct streams. "The Scamander" (says M. de Chevalier, Chap. IX.) "is but a *rivulet*, of about "15 feet broad, and 3 deep."[z] Captain Francklin says (page 35) It is "limpid and comparatively deep; running "in a channel 12 to 20 feet wide; till we lost it, in a morass." And the same again, page 40. The entire length of its course, from its fountains to the sea, is only 8 miles: and to what breadth soever it may spread out, in the marsh below, the size of the channel, above, must determine the volume of water. How, then, can *this* river pass for the *Scamander* of Homer; who styles it in different places, "*aweful flood :*" "*gulphy stream,*"—"*vortiginous ; from Jove derived.*"— "*swift* "*Scamander,*"—"*eddy whirling flood*"—"*dizzy stream,*"—all implying depth, capacity, and rapidity? And the effects described, are those produced by an occasional and furious torrent, at one season; as when Achilles combats it, in lib. xxi. v. 240: (Cowper, v. 283). But the battle in its bed, previous to its swelling, is descriptive of such a river as the Mender, in its *low state*; the indentations, or hollows in its

[y] Three hundred feet of breadth for the bed, seems to be the acknowledged dimensions; taken generally. Dr. Clarke says 130 *yards* at the bridge of Koumkala; 200 feet at the fords.

[z] It may be said, that if the Bounarbashi was the river in which the Virgin dedicated herself to the god *Scamander*, it would have been difficult for her to appear in it with decency; and one is equally at a loss to know, how Julia could have been exposed to the danger of drowning in such a stream!

lofty banks, serving to conceal the fugitives. (lib. xxi, v. 25."
" So lurk'd the trembling Trojans in the caves of Xanthus'
" aweful flood." (Cowper, v 32.)

But, independent of its *narrow dimensions*, the *description*
of the Bounarbashi River (by Capt. Francklin, p. 35, & 40)
does not give any such ideas. It is rather the reverse of
gulphy, aweful, or *deeply imbedded :* for its character, taken
at large, seems to partake more of the *beautiful,* than the
terrific. It cannot be *deep seated,* because the country
adjacent to its course, above its *former* conflux with the
Mender, is generally a marsh. Moreover, a stream that has
nearly the same body of water in it, at all times (springing
from the Plain, and having no adjuncts : or that can only
be affected by the rain water that falls near its banks,) has
no *use* for a *deep* bed ; which belongs only to a stream that
varies much in its bulk ; and which, oftentimes, requires a
more capacious bed than at others. Such *have* the Mender
and Shimar, but *not* the Bounarbashi.ₐ

When Priam crossed the Scamander in his way to the
tent of Achilles, no difficulty occurs ; but when Achilles
crossed it, during the battle and pursuit, it is an aweful flood :
agreeing with the Mender, in its different states.

The circumstance of the elm tree, which falling, served
as a bridge for Achilles, over the Scamander, has been
directly applied to the Bounarbashi River. But a *tall elm*
was not required for a rivulet of 12 to 20 feet wide !

ᵃ Captain Francklin applies a very characteristic phrase to the Bounarbashi
River (pages 33 and 35), which is, " *deeply embower'd :*" the banks being
covered with sedges, marsh-mallows, tamarisks, and rushes. He remarks, that
these often concealed the water from his view.

The truth appears to be, that the river bed was, at that time, only *filling*.[b]

The *Simoïs* bears a much smaller part than the *Scamander* in the transactions in the Iliad : but when spoken of, it appears to have much of the character of the *Scamander* : that is, *a mountain torrent*. The difference seems to be, that it is smaller ; and that its bed was not so frequently filled as that of the other[c] But the constant recurrence of the *Scamander*, implies that the warfare lay chiefly on that side, where the Plain was broadest, according to Demetrius : and as this agrees with the actual topography, it furnishes a presumptive proof of the identity of the *Mender* with the *Scamander*.

When the *Simoïs* is swoln, in lib. xii. v. 22, (Cowper, v. 28), it is only in common with *all* the other rivers of Ida, that is overflows and sweeps the Plain :

[b] Perhaps the Scamander of Homer is never more characteristically marked, than on occasion of the Trojan fugitives plunging into it, previous to its great flood : (lib. xxi. v. 7.)

——————————————— " Other part
" Push'd down the sides of Xanthus, headlong plung'd
" With dashing sound, into his dizzy stream."—
— " They, struggling, shriek'd, in silver eddies whirl'd." (Cowper, v. 9.)
And Lycaon, in v. 52,
——————————————— " fatigu'd
" Till his knees fail'd with toil to reach the land." (Cowper, v. 61.)

Can these descriptions be supposed to refer to a stream of three feet in depth, and sixteen to twenty in breadth, and not subject to floods ?

[c] For it cannot be supposed otherwise, than that the *Simoïs* lay in the way between the Grecian Camp and Troy : and yet it is never said to have opposed an obstacle to the free passage of the Greeks, during their warfare.

———— " Simoïs, whose banks with
" Helmets and with shields were strewed."

When in lib. xxi. v. 308, (Cowper, v. 363) the Scamander
calls for the aid of the Simoïs, to overwhelm Achilles, with
his torrents, it shews, indeed, the Simoïs to be a torrent
much of the same nature with the Mender, only smaller:
and with its bed *empty*, whilst that of the Scamander was
full, or filling. And even this comparative state of the two
rivers, furnishes a presumptive proof, in favour of the identity
of the Mender, with the *Scamander*, and the Shimar with
the *Simoïs*. For the Mender, receiving supplies from various
and remote quarters; and which have amongst them, at the
same time, different kinds of weather, will oftener be filled
than the Shimar; which springing from the *neighbouring
skirt* of Ida, depends for its supplies on a very limited tract.
(See the Map, N°. VI.)

When the Scamander thus calls for the aid of the Simoïs,
the bed of this latter must either have been *empty*, or very
scantily filled: or the words could have no meaning. If
then, with M. Chevalier, the Bounarbashi is to be taken
for the Scamander, and the Mender for the Simoïs, how
could so formidable a flood be produced by the Bounarbashi
alone, whose waters are ordinarily contained within a channel
of 20 feet wide, and 3 in depth? Let it be remembered,
however, that A FLOOD WAS PRODUCED; and that, without
the aid of the Simoïs: therefore it could only have been
produced by the Mender.[d]

[d] The author cannot but regard this particular as of great importance to the
question: and therefore requests the reader to keep it in mind, as he advances.

There are no *data* in Homer for the place of the ancient conflux of the two rivers. Demetrius, it has been shewn, places it near *New Ilium*: by which it is proved that the Scamander must have kept a different course from the present; emptying itself more towards *Rhœteum*.

It would appear that Achilles, during his pursuit of the Trojans, after the last battle (lib. xxi.) crossed the Scamander; and that *below* the conflux, be it where it might: otherwise by what *road* could the Simoïs have come to it, when called? The *fords* of the Scamander, should have been near the Sepulchre of Ilus, (according to Priam's rout, in lib. xxiv.)[c]; but there is no reason to suppose that Achilles crossed so low down. He was in pursuit of a flying enemy, whose army had been drawn up, with its right extending to the Monument of Ilus (for it was on the *Throsmos*, lib. xx. v. 3.);[f] and who had probably been pursued to some distance, in the way towards Troy, before Achilles crossed the river. But there is a circumstance more in point, to the conflux: Juno and Minerva alight *at the conflux* (lib. v., v. 774)[g] with an intent *to interfere* in the first battle; in which the Trojan army was drawn up at the Monument of *Batiœa*, (or *Myrinna*), which stood in front of Troy, and not far from the

[c] Moreover, Hector, when disabled by a blow of a stone, discharged by Ajax, at the first attack of the rampart and ships, (lib. xiv. v. 434) is carried to the side of the Scamander; and revived by pouring some of its water on his face. The *fords* of the river were said to be at this place: and as the main object of visiting it, appears to have been to obtain water readily (as they carried him no farther) it may be concluded that the fords were not far from the scene of action; *i. e.* the Grecian Camp, and Fleet; nor, of course, from the *Tumulus* of *Ilus.*

[f] Cowper, v. 3.   [g] Id. v. 872.

Scæan Gate. One must conclude that the Poet would set them down, *near* the field, in which they came to take part: and consequently, that the conflux intended by Homer would probably have not been lower down, than the present one at Kalifatli.

It must be acknowledged, that he affords no such proofs of the identity of the Simoïs, with the Shimar, by its peculiar character, as he does of the Scamander, by means of a comparison with the Mender: and by an absolute contrast, which is found between it, and the Bounarbashi River. But other circumstances afford internal evidence, which may satisfy us.

No notice is taken of any fords of the *Simoïs,* or even of crossing that river, at any time, between the Grecian Camp and Troy. Hence, it must be concluded, that it was low in its bed, during the battles and marches: and which certainly happened during the last battle, by the circumstances before mentioned. Nor is there any intimation given by our modern travellers, of the swelling of this river, otherwise than by *report,* and by appearances; and it may therefore be concluded, that it seldom swells, except in the winter; a season in which none of them have visited the Troad.[h] It may also be recollected, that the warfare happened during the summer season.

Upon the whole, then, it may be allowed, that the characters and descriptions of the Rivers; the position of the Hill

[h] Dr. Clarke's description of it, Vol, 2, p. 96, shews that its nature was that of a *torrent:* for though stagnant, it was not every where fordable: but like most of those water-courses which only run, during the draining off of the rain-water, its bed was formed of deep pits and shallows.

of Atchekui, taken for the *Kalli-colone*; with that of the *Tumulus,* inferred to be that of Myrinna ; the great width of the Plain, between the Mender and the Shimar, compared with that between the Mender and Bounarbashi (and which, moreover, has no *Tumulus* within it, as the history requires) ; all these circumstances combined, seem to afford evidence in favour of the idea, that Homer intended the same Plain for the scene of the Iliad, with that assigned to it by Demetrius.

The TWO SPRINGS before the *Scæan* Gate, described by Homer, were not recognized by Demetrius : but he could not, however, be supposed ignorant of the *series* of springs, at the foot of Bounarbashi Hill ; *two* of which have been selected by M. de Chevalier.

Homer certainly did not intend to describe a *hot* spring ; but one that was luke-warm, or *tepid ;* though surely of a warmer temperature, than is expressed by 62 or 64 of Fahrenheit's scale (for all the different reports fall between these numbers.[i])

" One of these springs," (says the Poet,) " flowed of a luke-warm temperature, diffusing smoke, as from a burning fire : the other was in the summer time, like hail, snow, or congealed water. Close to these fountains, there were broad and beautiful cisterns of marble, where, in peaceful times, the wives and fair daughters of the Trojans, used to wash their resplendent garments."[k] Lib. xxiv. v. 147, *et seq.*

[i] Mr Hawkins reports - - 63 to 64 ⎫
    Captain Hayes - - - 64 ⎬ 63¼
    Dr. Clarke - - - 62 ⎭
    Mr. Hobhouse, since - - 61

[k] Doctor Gillies.

Here, then, the Poet intended to mark a *striking contrast* between the two springs: but, by every account,[1] not only the two, selected, but the whole series, are precisely of the same temperature; that is, *cold*.

Mr. Hawkins says, that 63 to 64 was the temperature of all the springs which he examined: the water (says he) was " equally *cold* in them all." And Dr. Sibthorpe, at the same time, says of the reputed warm spring, " it communicated to us no sensation of heat." Edinb. Trans. Vol. IV. p. 114, and 115. This was in the month of April.

Most of the persons who have visited these springs, during the milder seasons, were *told* by the *natives*, that the reputed warm spring was *really warm* during the coldest part of the winter. However, it does by no means appear, that there is any difference in the temperature, between the summer and the winter seasons. For it seems by Mr. Gell, page 75, that Doctor Clarke tried it in the coldest weather of the year 1801; and he reports it to be 62. (Vol. II. page 110;) whilst Mr. Hawkins reports 63 to 64, in April. And, in effect, the different reports between April and November, cannot be said to differ from those, in the coldest part of the winter; when the difference amongst Thermometers is considered If any thing, they rather shew that the winter temperature is the coldest. M. de Chevalier indeed says (page 26) that in the latter end of September, he felt the water warm. Yet September is not a cold month in any climate.

[1] That is, by Mr. Hawkins, Doctor Sibthorpe, Mr. Gell, Doctor Clarke, Captain Hayes, Mr. Hobhouse, &c.

But is it to be conceived, that a deep-seated spring, cold in summer, should be warm in winter? If removed from the influence of the atmosphere, what should affect its temperature, *periodically?*

The truth probably is, that in the coldest part of winter the temperature of the atmosphere is *so much* colder than that of the reputed warm Spring, that the latter really feels comparatively warm to the touch; as also that a steam sometimes arises; which appearance may contribute as much towards exciting an idea of warmth, as the actual temperature. And as *one* of the Springs *alone*, emits a steam, whilst both are of the same temperature, at the place of discharge; this may well happen from the circumstance of its waters being confined within a narrower space, after ejection; and therefore, for a time, preserve nearly their original temperature: whilst those of the other Spring, being spread out, over a wide bason, receive the action of the air on their surface, and become colder. So that the water, as fast as it is ejected, is mixed with a large mass of colder water. For these appear to be the circumstances of the *two* Springs, usually denominated, the *warm*, and the *cold*. The experiments were made by immersing the thermometer in the mouths of the Springs.

There are not wanting, in every temperate climate, cold Springs that send up a steam in the cold weather of winter. The common remark, that certain springs are *cold* in *summer*, and *warm* in *winter*, is well known, and accounted for.

Still it may be objected, and with truth, that these are *above* the temperature of ordinary springs, in the parallel of 40°. For in the same parallel, near the sea-coast of Italy, their temperature is only 57°.[m] (At New York they are said to be from 54 to 56 only.)[n] Hence the Springs at Bounar-bashi, are at least 6 degrees higher than might have been expected from the temperature, proper to ordinary Springs in that parallel.

But it appears that certain *deep seated* Springs are found to be considerably warmer, than those which have their origin nearer to the surface; whatsoever the cause may be. This may be illustrated by what is known in this island, and particularly in the environs of the metropolis; where several wells have of late years been worked, through the entire depth of the *stratum* of blue clay; which extends from 250 to 300 feet, at least, below the level of the Thames. Under this *stratum* is found a kind of *abyss*, containing sand and water; whose temperature, (at least, when it arrives at the surface,) is several degrees warmer than that of the *superficial* Springs; which is known to be regulated by the *mean temperature* of the incumbent atmosphere. This, according to the Register kept at the Royal Society's apartments in London, is about $50\frac{1}{2}$ degrees of Fahrenheit: and is perhaps only a fraction lower, by the *registers* in general, throughout this quarter of the Island.[o]

[m] Sir Charles Blagden.

[n] An experiment of Dr. Nocth's, reported by the late Dr. John Hunter, in his " Observations on the Diseases of the Army in Jamaica :" &c. &c. p. 283.

[o] The mean temperature in London, is deduced from a register of Mr. Six's thermometer, kept in the open air: the mean of 16 years was $50\frac{1}{2}$ degrees. Another series of observations, in the same place, with a common thermometer, during 23 years, was $50\frac{3}{4}$. That of Mr. Barker, at Lyndon, in Rutlandshire, gave the mean at a small fraction lower than Mr. Six's: a result, not at all improbable.

The springs of several wells, of the kind which penetrate the *stratum* of clay, are found to be 56; which is therefore 5 or 6 degrees at least, above the mean temperature of the incumbent atmosphere. One of these was dug by Mr. B. Vulliamy, in 1794,[p] and still continues to overflow, though nearly 330 feet in depth. A second is at Richmond; and a third is the famous well, dug by Sir Thomas Page, in 1782, at Sheerness.[q] There are others, whose temperatures are not known to the Author: in particular that one of the great depth of 563 feet, dug by Earl Spencer, at Wimbledon Park.

The Springs at Bounarbashi, then, taken at the mean of the different reports, which is about 63; whilst the mean temperature of the ordinary springs in that parallel, is reckoned at 57, or six degrees lower; afford an example of much the same kind, with the *deep-seated* Springs here; and as they are said to be in Holland. And hence, there is nothing uncommon in the circumstance, as it relates to Bounarbashi: since a *stratum* of sand and water, under the like circumstances with the abovementioned, may also exist in that place.[r]

Dr. Hunter, however, from a register kept by Lord Charles Cavendish, in London, deduces a mean temperature of 49,196. (Obs. p. 279.) And it appears from several experiments, that the temperature of what may be called *superficial* springs, (in contradistinction to those from below the blue clay,) is about $49\frac{1}{2}$. It is remarked that " the observations from which the mean is taken, must " generally contain more of the extremes of heat than of cold; as the former " happen in the day time, and the latter in the night; in consequence of which " they will often escape notice." (Obs. p. 279.)

[p] See Phil. Trans. for 1797.   [q] Ibid. for 1784.

[r] Dr. Shaw reports that the wells in *Wadreag*, on the edge of the Great

But to return more immediately to our subject, it is a CONTRAST that is sought for, as well as a WARM SPRING; and those in question, are both of the same temperature: that is, COLD. For Mr. Hawkins has said, that the water was " *equally cold in them all:*" and Dr. Sibthorpe, that the reputed warm Spring " *communicated to them, no sensation of heat.*"

It must at the same time be allowed, that the appearance of the reputed warm Spring, in respect of its massy blocks of marble, and other stones, is very imposing; and the circumstance of the one smoking in winter, whilst the other does not, (if this really be true), is likewise calculated to persuade ordinary people, that one Spring is *warm*, whilst the other is cold. But appearances cannot supply the want of WARMTH, in one, to form a *contrast* with the other.

There is little doubt, but that on the report of these Springs (however fallacious that report may have been) M. de Chevalier's argument to prove that the position of Bounarbashi, was that of Troy, has chiefly rested: and which, even repeated experiments, proving that the temperature of both is exactly alike, have not yet afforded conviction.

Had they presented any *contrast* in point of temperature, they might have *passed* for the objects *intended* in the Poem: in which case, it might have been supposed, that the Poet

African Desert, are dug to *an amazing* depth: and that " the water, *mixed with fine sand,* springs up suddenly, and sometimes fatally, to the workmen. And that the people call this *abyss, the Sea below Ground.*" (Travels in Barbary, page 135.) The temperature is not reported. Exactly the same kind of wells are dug in Holland; where the abyss is also called " *the Sea under the Land.*"

  * Mr. Hobhouse, in his late Travels says, " *only not chill.*" Page 761.

had selected his objects, without much regard to their topographical consistency; but merely to their bearing on the
action of the Poem. But as so many other particulars of
the Topography, coincide with the historical part of it, one
naturally expects consistency in this also: especially as the
position of *Troy*, *the Kalli-colone*, &c. have so close a connexion with that of the Springs.[t]

Although there seems to be little difficulty, in identifying
the two Rivers that bounded the Plain of the Troad; or in
fixing the *upper* parts of their courses; yet the changes that
must necessarily have taken place in the *lower* and *alluvial*
parts, render it difficult to fix their particular line of course,
or that of the sea-shore at the head of the Bay; at any given
time. However, reasoning from appearances, and from
analogy, the Mender (*Scamander;* meaning the confluent
river) must, in a course of ages, have varied its bed,
throughout the whole space, between the two Promontories
of *Sigæum* and *Rhœteum*. The *deserted* channels, remarked
by Mr. Gell, and by Mr. Carlyle, are in proof of it: and the
history of every river that forms any considerable alluvions,
furnishes examples of a like kind.

One can only endeavour, therefore, in the first instance, to

[t] Most of our readers are undoubtedly aware, that it is by no means an
uncommon case, to find hot and cold Springs, very close to each other.
Therefore the mere existence of such, even in the quarter of the Troad, if
unaccompanied with any of the other objects, belonging to the description of
the place, would not afford complete conviction. The Author has seen them in
Bengal so very near together, that a frog leapt from the cold one into the other,
which was *scalding hot*.

approximate the general position of the *Ancient Shore* of the Bay, at some given period of history ; as for instance, in the time of Demetrius, or of Strabo : and to deduce from thence, according to the *acknowledged measure of recedence* of the sea ; checked by reason and analogy ; the position of the same shore, and Camp of the Greeks, at the time of the Trojan War. And finally, if, in reference to such an approximated position of the shore, a *tumulus* can be found, answering to that of ILUS ; we may be enabled to adjust, in a general way, the ancient course of the lower part of the Scamander, (that is, the Scamander and Simoïs united) which had a close connexion with this *tumulus*, in the history of the transactions of the Iliad. And, as a necessary consequence, the position of the *Throsmos*, or rising ground, on which the Trojan army encamped, at the attack of the Grecian wall, may be approximated : together with the places of the fields of battle ; and of the transactions recorded in the ten consecutive Books of the Iliad, from the *eighth* to the *seventeenth*, both inclusive.

In the course of this enquiry, the Author has often found it necessary to enter into very minute details, in order to illustrate more fully the History of the Poem. Repetitions also, were found to be unavoidable, in the attempt to render each separate head of enquiry more distinct.

SECTION II.

CONCERNING THE POSITION OF THE CAMP AND RAMPART OF THE GREEKS.

The Promontories of Sigæum *and* Rhœteum *not* named *by Homer, but identified by Pliny—Accretion of Soil, at the Mouth of the* Scamander, *over-rated; both by Demetrius, and by Modern Writers—Proved by the* mode *of progress to which it is necessarily confined—Idea of the* Bay, *and Station of the* Fleet—Tumulus *of the* Greeks, *slain in the* first Battle—Tumulus *of* Achilles, *and of* Patroclus—*of* Ajax— *Arrangement of the Ships, the Camp, and the Rampart, or Wall of Defence—Extent of the Bay, much over-rated by all the Ancients.*

This, and the three succeeding articles; namely, the Monument of *Ilus;* the *lower part* of the course of the *Scamander;* and the *Throsmos;* having a close connexion with each other, in respect of position; and mutually throwing light on each other; are discussed in succession: and in the order in which they are mentioned.

The Grecian Fleet was drawn up on the shore, between two promontories; which although not named, are clearly shewn to be those of *Sigæum* and *Rhœteum.* And in the intermediate space, was the mouth of the *Scamander*, or *Xanthus.* See the Iliad. lib. xiv. v. 36, for the Promontories.[a]

[a] Cowper, v. 42.

The mouth of the river is constantly implied to be situated between them; but not expressed in *terms*, in the ILIAD.

Sigæum is a geographical position, concerning which, there can be no doubt: since its Promontory, which separates the *Hellespont* from the *Ægean Sea*, is universally recognised in the southern Cape of the *Dardanêlles*. One of the Tumuli[x] on this Cape, regarded as the Monument of ACHILLES, was marked by the Town of *Achilleum*, adjacent to it: the other Promontory must of course be that of *Rhæteum*; whose *Tumulus* is ascribed to AJAX, with equal authority.

Pliny (lib. v. c. 30.) says, " There has been ACHILLEUM, " a town near the Tomb of ACHILLES, first built by the " Mitylenéans, and afterwards rebuilt by the Athenians ; " where his fleet had been placed, near *Sigæum*. There has " been an ÆANTE′UM also ; built by the Rhodians at the " other *corner* [of the Bay], where the Sepulchre of AJAX " is ; and where the Station of his Fleet had been, 30 stadia " from *Sigæum*."

Herodotus also mentions *Achilleum*. (*Terpsichore*, c. 94.)

So that it appears to have been the received opinion of ancient times, that these were the sepulchres of those heroes. And it seems by no means too great an assumption, to fix their stations in the line of battle, in situations correspondent to the stations of their ships, and to their respective monuments.

The accumulation of alluvial matter, *here*, must have been so considerable, in the course of 30 centuries, as to defy all

---

[x] There being two : the other is supposed, probably with reason, to be the monument of PATROCLUS.

attempts to determine, otherwise than in a very general way, the line of the sea coast, at the time when the Greeks encamped on it.

But Strabo (page 598) informs us, from Demetrius, that in his time (nearly two centuries before our æra) the sea-coast was 12 stadia distant from New Ilium. And Pliny (lib. v. c. 30) says a Roman mile and half; which probably arose from his erroneously converting the Grecian itinerary stades into Roman miles, at the rate of 8 to a mile, which was his usual practice: therefore the report of Demetrius is to be preferred; as he probably reckoned by Grecian stades.[y]

It has appeared (see above page 41), that there is little doubt, respecting the general position of *New Ilium;* which stood on the hill, or rising ground, situated about a mile to the south-east of Koum-kui.[z] And it is collected from Strabo (page 599) that the city extended *to the brow* of the hill, and not *beyond it:* for that appears to be the meaning of the passage:[a] and the ruins now found on the hill, are described

[y] As the Grecian and Roman stades differed in the proportion of about 6 to 7, the Roman mile and a half would be equal to about 14 Grecian stades, of 700 to a degree.

The *mean* itinerary stade of the Greeks, according to the authorities cited in "the Geography of Herodotus," page 31, is equal to the $\frac{1}{718}$ th part of a degree. Strabo's scale is 700 to a degree, and the Roman 600; or 8 to one of their miles. There can be little doubt but that Demetrius reckoned by Grecian stades; as the Roman could not well have been in use there, at that early period.

[z] See in the Map, the compartments N°. I. and II. Also Mr. Gell's Plan, N°. XLV.

[a] It is, when he was attempting to prove that the Ilium of his time was not the ancient Troy. He says, "Hector could not have been pursued round about "New Ilium, because of the nature of the ground." One must conclude, therefore, that the ground went with a steep declivity, from the foot of the wall.

to extend *to its brow*; towards Koum-kui, and the Mender. Still the shore would probably have been deeply indented, as at present, by the deserted beds of the river, and inequalities in the *new formed* land : therefore only *a kind of mean* can be taken, for the whole line of the *then* coast; which may be supposed to have been nearly parallel to the present one. (See N°. I. and II.)

The brow of the hill which forms the site of New Ilium is at present *nearly* two British miles from the nearest alluvial shore; which is that at the entrance of In-Tepé-Azmah, or the inlet to the Tumulus of Ajax (the Port of *Æantéum*); that is, equal to 19 stades, and upwards, instead of the 12 stades, in the time of Demetrius. Taking the 12 stades at Strabo's scale of 700 to a degree, we have one British mile, and nearly a quarter, for that part of the shore, that was opposite to New Ilium, in the time of Demetrius; about 1000 years in round numbers, after the Trojan war; 2000 short of the present time. Demetrius also states (Strabo, page 598) that half of the beforementioned space; that is, 6 stadia of the 12; had been added, by accretion, since the Trojan war. But this appears excessive, and therefore improbable, when the subject is examined closely; and therefore ought not to be received, without great allowance for exaggeration : as being, probably, no more than the vague report of the place. But the report of the distance of the shore from New Ilium, in the time of Demetrius, rests on a different foundation; and is consequently important and interesting. Admitting, therefore, that the coast has gained nearly $\frac{3}{4}$ of a mile (or full 7 stadia of Strabo's scale) in 2000 years, it ought, at the same rate, to have gained no more than $3\frac{1}{2}$ stades, instead of the 6, reported; if under similar circumstances. And according to this rough kind of estimate, the shore, in the time of the Trojan war, should have been $8\frac{1}{2}$ stades from the site of New Ilium: or somewhat more than $\frac{4}{5}$ of an English mile.

We are apt to reckon too fast, in the calculation of the increase of alluvial shores; and sometimes do not reflect, that although the surface of a country, and the river banks, may be composed of alluvial matter, yet that it may be nothing more than *strata* of such matter, laid upon the original soil; as the country rises by the repeated depositions of floods. For the operations of *forming new* land, and of *raising the old*, necessarily go on together.

There is, moreover, given by Demetrius, a measure of 20 stadia, between New Ilium and the *Naustathmus*, where the Scamander is said to have *then* discharged itself. (Strabo, page 598) On the application of this distance, to the Map, it will be found, that whatsoever may have happened elsewhere, the coast cannot have gained $\frac{3}{4}$ of a mile, in *that part;* although for want of good *landmarks*, the ancient measures cannot be applied, *accurately*. In the sequel, we trust that it will be made to appear probable, that the *Tumulus* at the Bridge of Koum-kala, stood near, or adjacent to, the Grecian wall: which, if admitted, the accretion must have been much less *there*, than between New Ilium and the sea; according to the report of Demetrius: and, in fact, it can scarcely be doubted, that the accretion has been much greater towards *Rhæteum*, than *Sigæum;* for reasons that will presently appear.

If the measure of accretion arising from the depositions

of many other rivers, in various parts of the world, was to
be applied to the Mender, it would only be calculated to
mislead.   For the Mender, in respect of its *whole* bed, is
only an *occasional* river, or torrent : and therefore, is not
constantly bringing down the matter of alluvion, like the
Ganges, Mæander, and other such rivers.   Here is a space
of a mile and half, in *breadth,* along the coast of the Bay, to
be filled up, by a stream, whose *bed,* indeed, is 300 feet in
breadth, but whose *stream* is very commonly so low, as to
be crossed *dry shod.*[b]   Were it constantly filled, its operation
would be greatly accelerated ; but still could only proceed
in the same *mode* as at present ; which is, by adding *narrow
tongues* or *slips* of alluvion, on each side of its bed ; which it
pushes forward into the sea :[c]   And if the mass of alluvion,
created, was equal to the breadth of the whole river bed
(300 feet) it would require 26 such *slips,* or *tongues* breadth-
wise, to fill up the space.   So that, in order to form *one*
foot of new land in the sea, along the whole breadth of the
Bay, the River Mender must advance a quantity of alluvion,
equal to 26 feet, on a single slip.   And had 6 stades, equal
to more than 3000 feet, been added in 1000 years, a border
of more than 3 feet annually, must have been added, across
the whole extent of a mile and half : which is equal to the
formation of *a piece of land* in the sea, 300 feet by 80, in
each year ; which is not to be credited ; since the bed of
the river is only occasionally filled.   It is a proportion beyond

[b] This is the expression made use of, by Doctor Chandler, in particular. One
must conclude that they passed over upon stepping-stones. (Travels, p. 41.)

[c] See the progress of alluvion, in the geographical system of Herodotus ;
chapter xviii.

what the Ganges, with all its floods, and matter of alluvion ;
and with an *unceasing* stream, accomplishes.

HOMER gives an idea of an open, winding shore, or bay,
only ; *not a port :* it is to the description of others, that we
are indebted, for the notice of a Port of the Achæans ;
which may, or may not, have existed during the time of the
Trojan war.[d] Possibly, the same openings, now in existence,
may have existed in the same lines, from remote antiquity,
though removed lower down, as the coast was prolonged :
for they were probably *deserted beds* of the *Scamander*, which
had wandered from one part of the bay, to another.

It only appears necessary, for the present purpose, to suppose a *general outline* of shore, or beach, of a curvilinear
form, extending between the high lands of the Capes of
Sigæum and *Rhœteum ;* and at $8\frac{1}{2}$ [e] stades from the *brow* of
the hill of New Ilium ; or somewhat more than $\frac{4}{5}$ of an
English mile. This line, of course, will mark the supposed
range of the Grecian fleet, which was drawn up on the shore,
in several lines, *across* the head of the Bay.   A reference to
the Plan Nº. II. will shew, that the sea, at that time, must

---

[d] Strabo, pages 595 and 598 : and Pliny, lib. v. c. 30.

Some have applied the term *Achæan Port* to the *whole Bay*, at the head of
which the fleet was drawn up.   But the same authority which places this Port
at 12 stadia from *New Ilium*, gives the *Naustathmus* at 20 : so that there were
two distinct Ports in the Bay : and the *Bay itself*, of course, was out of the
question, as a *Port.*

[e] That is, $3\frac{1}{2}$ being taken from 12, the distance of the shore from New Ilium,
in the time of Demetrius.

have washed the whole western face of the hill, which forms the broad Promontory of *Rhœteum*: and, of course, must have *approached*, or even *entered*, the mouth of the Valley of *Thymbra* : (now Thymbrek, or Dumbrek.) And from this point, we must conceive the shore of the Bay, to have extended to the W. N. W. (or nearly parallel to the present coast,) *towards* the Promontory of *Sigæum*, and the *Tumulus* of Achilles ; terminating at the edge of the *high* ground, which forms the *present* western bank of the Mender. Such a line would, of course, have fallen very far *within* the *present* shore ; which can hardly be said to form a bay.

On the above supposition, it is not unreasonable to regard with Mr. Gell, (Troy, page 45) the *Tumulus* near the bridge of Koum-kala, as the one described by Homer, as the universal tomb of the Greeks, slain in the *first* battle before Troy ; and whose bodies were collected and removed thither for that purpose.[f] To countenance this supposition, we have the *Tumuli* of Achilles and Patroclus, exactly in a line with the other; and in the very neighbourhood of their stations, in the line of battle : but advanced towards the termination of the Promontory, for the sake of placing them in a more conspicuous situation;[g] as we see that of Ajax, in a corresponding situation, adapted to *his* station in the same line.

It has been remarked, that the greatest accumulation of

---

[f] Iliad, lib. vii. v. 430: Cowper, v. 452.

[g] Odyssey, lib. xxiv. v. 80. *et seq.*

     " On a tall Promontory, shooting far
     " Into the spacious Hellespont, that all
     " Who live, and who shall yet be born, may view,
     " Thy record, even from the distant wave."   (Cowper, v. 94, *et. seq.*)

alluvion, has been in the quarter of *Rhœteum*. This may be accounted for, in the first place, by the longer continuance of the course of the Mender there. But another, and principal cause, may have been, the operation of filling up the Bay, by the new formed land ; which brought the river current, into more immediate contact with the current of the *Hellespont :* so that a great part of the matter of alluvion, was diverted from its former place of deposit, and hurried away into the *Ægean* Sea. The advance of the mouth of the river, towards *Sigæum*, would have a like tendency ; by removing the cause of alluvion farther from the side of *Rhœteum*.

Connected with the above *Tumulus* of the Greeks, was the *right flank* [h] of the wall or rampart: for in lib. vii. v. 337, it is said,

   ———————— " to the tomb *adjoined*
 " We will construct high tow'rs for the defence
 " Of us, and of our fleet." (Cowper, v. 349.)

To a reader who has been accustomed to regard the quantity of accretion as in a manner *indefinite,* this Tumulus may appear to be too low down, towards the sea. There is, however, *no other* in this quarter, save the one near the former conflux of the Mender and Bounarbashi Rivers: and which is much *too far removed* from the shore of the Hellespont; as we also conceive that of Koum-kui to be. It is impossible, at this day, to guess what circumstances may

---

[h] That is, the *right*, as it respected the Greeks within the wall. Had it stood on the *left*, it would probably have been mentioned, during the attack on the *left*, by Hector.

have determined the choice of position, for this commanding work; which was at once to serve as a tomb, and place of arms: but it may possibly have been, to command the water-course, when the Bounarbashi River may be supposed to have flowed singly through the bed, since occupied by the joint waters of that river and the Mender: and being itself a mere rivulet, and not subject to great swellings, was harmless, in a military view: and at the same time would prove very convenient to that part of the camp; as the Mender to the opposite quarter of it.

On this Beach, then, of which we have attempted to approximate the position, the Grecian fleet was drawn up, in lines, or rows, (probably 4 or 5) parallel to the head of the Bay, and with their sterns towards the land :[i] the rampart rising, at a convenient distance, beyond the innermost row. (Iliad, lib. xiv. v. 30:)

> " For, distant from the dang'rous field, the Greeks
> Had rang'd their barks beside the hoary deep;
> The foremost next the Plain, and at the sterns
> Of that exterior line had built the wall."

(Cowper, v. 34.)

[i] This circumstance alone, seems to prove how very different the form of the ancient ships, was from the present ones. Modern ships swim much deeper by the stern than by the head ; and are therefore always placed with their sterns to seaward. (See also lib. xiii. v. 762.)

The same mode of placing the stern, appears in Herodotus, Clio, c. 1. "These females, standing near the stern of the vessel,"—that is, on the shore: because after they were seized, they were " carried on board." The Phœnician merchandize had been exposed for sale : the place would doubtless have been somewhat removed from the margin of the sea; and therefore the stern must have been towards the land, and the market, a little within it.

Streets of tents were placed *between* the rows of ships :[k] and it may be supposed, as a matter of course, that a large body of troops was encamped between the ships and the rampart.

It appears by Mr. Gell's Plan (N°. XLV) that the space between the high lands of *Sigæum* and *Rhæteum*, across the head of the Bay, is *now* about a mile and half, or rather more : and in M. Kauffer's Plan, about the same : and was probably much the same anciently, although over-rated by Pliny and Strabo.[l]

Of this space, it may be supposed that a mile and quarter, or more, was applicable to the purpose of placing the ships, and of covering them with a rampart. The Greeks would not, certainly, have taken within their camp, the course of the *great torrent, Scamander*, so as to hazard a separation of their force, by its sudden swelling : an event that happened suddenly and unexpectedly, during Achilles's pursuit of the Trojans, after the last battle.

Had the Beach even admitted of placing the whole fleet in one line,[m] this would have been incompatible with its defence ; since such a line, containing nearly 1200 vessels,

[k] Iliad, lib. xv. v. 656 : Cowper, v. 770.

[l] Strabo (p. 595,) says that the distance across from one Promontory to the other, is 60 stades : Pliny, (lib. v. c. 33) 30 stades. But no more than 2 British miles, or about 20 stades, arise, on the plans of Messrs. Kauffer and Gell, between the *Tumulus* of Ajax, and that of Patroclus : nor more than $2\frac{1}{2}$ miles, or about 25 stades, between the *Tumulus* of Ajax, and the Town of Jenishehr (*Sigæum*). So that even the lowest of the ancient statements (Pliny's) is either in excess, or corrupted ; although M. de C. praises his accuracy in this place.

[m] — " Spacious though it were, *the shore alone*

" *That fleet sufficed not*, incommoding much

" The people ; wherefore they had rang'd the ships

could not have been less than 4 or 5 miles in length : but a mile and quarter, or more, of rampart, might be commodiously defended, by such a force as the Greeks possessed ; or might have had on the spot.

The ships must have been drawn close to each other, side by side, in order to allow of Ajax's *striding* from one ship to another, during the attack, within the lines. And what was equally necessary, they were *propped* either with stones, or shores, to keep them upright ° This being the case, there must of necessity have been large intervals left at proper distances, for a regular and unobstructed communication, at all times, between the streets of the camp : and especially in the event of an attack ; as really happened. It may of course be supposed, that the whole of the mariners, and as

" *Line above line ascending,* and the bay
" Between both Promontories, all was filled."

Lib. xiv. v. 34. Cowper. v. 38.

The Catalogue of Homer (lib. ii.) contains 1183 to 1186 ships. Thucydides reckons them roundly at 1200 (lib. i.) : so that it may be concluded, that the general number has been handed down pretty accurately.

The words of this great historian, respecting the subject of the armament, are worthy of remark.

" Let it not be supposed, because of the smallness of the City of *Mycenæ,* (Agamemnon's capital) that the fleet was less numerous than the Poets have represented ; and as Fame has reported it to have been—but rather suppose that the expedition was even greater than any of the preceding ones ; although inferior to those of the present age."—(that of the *Peloponnesian* war.)

He then proceeds to state, that as Homer has given the scale of the largest and of the smallest vessels ; that is, of 120 men, and of 50, each ; the mean [at 85, giving 102,000 men] does not constitute such a force, considered as a joint effort of *all Greece,* as could be reckoned great. (Thucydides, lib. i. Smith's Trans.)

 • Iliad, lib. i. v. 487 ; and also xiv. v. 410. Cowper, 490, and 485, respectively.

many of the troops, besides, as could conveniently be accommodated, were lodged *in* the ships.

Such a disposition, together with the rampart and ditch, and the projecting towers beyond them; with an allowance for the spray of a small wave, clear of the outermost range of ships; cannot well be taken at a depth of less than 900 feet, from the Beach, to the outer edge of the ditch of the rampart. However, it may well be supposed that no part of the Grecian Camp, lay to the east of the Scamander: but rather that they would make use of it, to cover the *left* flank of their position. We now proceed to enquire into the position of the TUMULUS of ILUS; and of the line of course, and circumstances, of the LOWER PART OF THE SCAMANDER; as essentially bearing on it, and on the general subject.

M

[82]

SECTION III.

CONCERNING THE TUMULUS, OR MONUMENT OF ILUS.

The Mound at Koum-kui, discovered by Mr. Gell, *taken for the* Tumulus *of* Ilus—*has a close Connexion with the* Throsmos *and* Rampart—Trees *said to grow on the* Tumulus *of* Ilus *by Theophrastus and Pliny.*

It happens, that in the just mentioned position of the Grecian Camp, the Mound, or *Tumulus*, near the Village of Koum-kui, first noticed by Mr. Gell, would have been about four stadia, or somewhat more than $\frac{3}{8}$ of a British mile distant from, and nearly fronting, the left of the same camp, and its rampart or wall.

It is in proof that the Monument of Ilus stood in the quarter opposite to the station of Ajax; which is known to have been on the *left*, or in the eastern part of the camp, where Hector made his attack:ᴾ whereas, the Tumulus at the ancient conflux of the Mender and Bounarbashi Rivers, which has been taken for it, would have been on the *right* of the same camp, which was the station of Achilles; and which was not attacked. Neither would the distance suit; as it could not well have been within a mile and quarter of the nearest part of the Grecian camp.

ᴾ The proof of this particular will be found in the succeeding section (Nº. IV.) on the lower part of the course of the Scamander; with which it is more intimately connected.

If, then, we have conceived the matter justly, the *Tumulus* near Koum-kui, would agree to that of ILUS, in respect of the assumed position of the Grecian camp and wall.

Homer describes the Tomb of ILUS, as lying in the ordinary road from the Grecian camp to Troy, (lib. xi. v. 166; and xxiv. v. 349: Cowper, v. 202, and 438.) In the former place, the Trojans are described to have fled from their position on the *Throsmos*, which was near this tomb, "*through the middle of the Plain*, to reach the City" of Troy: and in the latter, Priam passed it, in his way between Troy and the tent of Achilles. Indeed, whether Troy be placed in the Plain, eastward of the Mender, or at Bounarbashi, this Tumulus lies equally in the way between the site of the camp, and the city. (See the Map, N°. II.: and Mr. Gell's Plan, No. XLV.)

The Tumulus at Koum-kui has the remains of columns on it: (Gell. p. 116.) but these evidently belonged to a structure of much later date, than that of the Trojan war. That of Ilus had a single column, or *stela* on it: for Paris is said to have sheltered himself behind *a* column during the battle, in lib. xi. v. 370, 505.[q] It is the only one in the Plain, that is represented to have had a column on it: others, however, might have been finished in the same manner; but there was no necessity for mentioning it.

Of this monument, Mr. Gell speaks as follows: page 116. It is "a mound of considerable magnitude.—There is "every reason to suppose it artificial; for it is perfectly "insulated, and stands on a dead flat, near the *dry channel.*

[q] "Behind a stately pillar of the tomb
Of ancient Ilus." (Cowper, v. 452.)

" The heap is *not lofty;* and appears to have been levelled,
" for the purpose of placing on its summit, some kind of
" edifice, of which 2 or 3 marble columns are the remains.—
" It seems too extensive to have been designed for a
" Tumulus."

Mr. Gell says, that it is *not lofty.* But whatsoever may
have been its original height, it ought to appear lower now;
not only from the levelling of its summit, but from the alluvions, which must have raised the general level of the Plain,
at its base. (See above, page 73.)

The Tumulus of Ilus in the Iliad, has a close connexion,
topographically, with the Camp of the Greeks; and also
with the *Throsmos,* or rising ground, on which the Trojans
formed their camp, during their warfare, near the rampart;
and no less with the *lower course* of the *Scamander.* For
whilst the army of Troy occupied with its *right,* a part of
the Valley of *Thymbra, Hector* held a council at the Sepulchre of Ilus; at no greater distance from his own camp,
than what served to remove him from its noise and tumult;
whilst, at the same time, the military musick, and *hum* of
the same camp, was *heard in that of the Greeks.* One may
conclude, that the space of 4 stadia mentioned above, equal
to $\frac{3}{8}$ of a British mile, or somewhat more; as the interval,
between the supposed place of the rampart of the Greeks,
and the Tumulus of Koum-kui; may be allowed to agree
with the circumstances of the history.

The reader, of course, will not apply to ancient warfare
the rules followed in the modern. The missile weapons of
the ancients, commanded a narrow space, compared with
those of the moderns: and therefore there is nothing

contradictory to reason and probability, in the fact of the Trojan army having taken their ground within hearing of the Greeks.

Whether the Tumulus lay in the *front*, or in the *rear* of the Trojan camp, is not known: but probably the latter. It is, however, of no great importance to the question, when it is recollected that Hector might have avoided the noise or tumult of the camp (the alleged object) by merely ascending the mound.

It must be acknowledged that, had the Monument of Ilus been entirely unconnected with the transactions at the fleet and rampart, one would naturally have expected it to have been situated much higher up, towards Troy. But the history is too pointed and precise, to admit of such a supposition; that is, admitting that the Poet confined himself to facts, in his geography. But even admitting the contrary, what was the use of carrying Hector a mile or two from his camp, at so critical a time, in order to introduce a mere classical image, at the expense of probability and propriety.[r]

*** Since the above was written, Doctor Clarke's second volume has announced two Tumuli, in the Plain between Kalifatli and New Ilium, which appear to have been unnoticed to this time. (See N°. I. and II.)

One of these, appears to stand at the opening of the Valley of the Shimar River: the other in the midst of the Plain,

[r] The warfare near the Grecian wall proves, by a number of instances, in which Paris is described to wound the Grecian chiefs with arrows, shot from the Tomb of Ilus, that Homer spoke of a position near that wall. See Iliad, lib. xi. v. 370, and 582: Cowper, v. 452, and 699.

between Koum-kui and Kalifatli; and to the north of the
latter. From this Tumulus, the Doctor had a view of the
coast, towards the mouth of the Mender: and it had two
oak trees growing on it.

It was remarked by Theophrastus and Pliny, that trees
grew on the Sepulchre of Ilus, near New Ilium. Pliny
(lib. xvi. c. 44), calls them *oaks;* and says, it was reported,
that they were coeval with the Tumulus. Dr. Chandler,
(Hist. Troy, p. 76, 77,) quotes Theophrastus, who speaks of
beeches growing there.

It is possible that the *Tumulus* so described by Dr. Clarke,
may be the one intended by those authors, for the Sepulchre
of Ilus. But had it been the one recorded by Homer, where
Hector held a council on the left of the Grecian camp, and
almost within hearing distance from it, the sea, at that time,
must have washed the western front of the hill of *New Ilium;*
and consequently, the *place* of the Vale of *Thymbra*, would
have been a bay of the sea.

But the Vale of *Thymbra*, at that moment, contained the
Trojan auxiliaries, the *Thracians, Lycians,* and *Carians;* who,
collectively, formed the right wing, and reached to the sea.
(See N°. II). This is proved by the speech of Dolon; and
the night adventure of Ulysses and Diomed. (lib. x. v. 271,
Cowper, v. 316.) If, then, this be the Tumulus in question, we must suppose Hector to have gone a mile and
half from his post, to attend a council of war, whilst the
enemy, in full force, was within hearing of his army. Yet
the history says no more, than that Hector, with all his chief
officers, retired to the Tomb of Ilus, in order to avoid the
noise of his own camp. (lib. x. v. 415: Cowper, v. 474.)

SECTION IV.

CONCERNING THE LOWER PART OF THE COURSE OF THE SCAMANDER.

The Scamander *must have entered the Sea, near* Rhœteum, *at the date of the* Trojan War.—*The* LEFT, *the side on which Hector fought, explained to mean the* left *of the* Grecian Camp.—Port *of the* Achæans, *the same with that of Æan-téum; but distinct from the* Naustathmus—Palæ Sca-mander *of Pliny—Attempt to reconcile the Statements of Strabo and Pliny, respecting the position of the Mouth of the* Scamander—*Karanlik, or the* closed *Port —* Thymbrius *River.*

The lower part of the course of the *Scamander* (that is, the *Scamander* and *Simoïs* united) next claims attention. This river ought, according to the history, to have ran by the *left*, that is, on the *east*, of the Grecian wall; the attack on the station of Ajax, near *Rhœteum*, being " on the LEFT; and also *beside the Scamander.*" Hector also, as we have seen, held a council at the Monument of Ilus; and that council was said to have been " *at the Scamander.*" Now, the *left* intended, could not have been the left of Hector's army; but, on the contrary, that of the Grecian camp and wall; when looking from thence, towards the field. For as Achilles and Ajax were posted at the opposite extremities of the Grecian line; and it being admitted on all hands, that

Achilles was placed on the side towards *Sigæum*, it must follow of course, that Ajax was on the side of *Rhœteum;* which was on the left, in respect of the *Grecian* army, and not of the *Trojan.*[s]

But as the Author is aware that the *left*, as applied to Hector, in this case, has been almost universally understood in these times, to mean the left of the Trojan army; and as such, has been quoted in support of systems of the Topography; it will be proper to adduce proofs of the contrary: in order to which, it will be necessary to enter largely into detail.

It has appeared, that the Tomb of ILUS, was close, or very near to, the ford, or ordinary *pass* over the *Scamander*, in the way between Troy and the Grecian camp. (See above, page 59, note). Priam came to *a river*, after passing the Tomb of Ilus, on his way *to* the Grecian camp: and on his return, is actually said to have forded the *Xanthus* (*Scamander*); doubtless, the same river to which *he came*, as well as *passed*), in his way out.[t]

Again, Hector, as we have seen, held a council, at the side of the *Scamander;*[u] which council is afterwards[x] said to have been at the Tomb of Ilus.   Consequently, the Tomb of Ilus was not only at the *side* of the *Scamander*, but near its *ford*, also.

It is also said, that Hector fought beside the Scamander;

[s] The reader is again referred to the Map, N°. II.
[t] Iliad, lib. xxiv. v. 349, and 693.   Cowper, v. 439, and 867.
[u] Lib. viii. v. 490: Cowper, v. 563.
[x] Lib. x. v. 415: Cowper, v. 473.

and ON THE LEFT OF ALL THE WAR.[y] It would have been perhaps, too much in the style of a gazette, to speak alternately, of the right and left of the different armies: therefore the Poet appears to give, as a permanent mode of distinction, and one that could not well be mistaken, afterwards, the LEFT of the Grecian wall and camp: at once, a fixed point; and the principal scene of warfare.

Moreover, it is very clearly shewn, that Achilles had his station on the RIGHT of the Grecian line, towards *Sigæum;* and Ajax on the LEFT, towards *Rhœteum;* and Agamemnon appears to have been in the CENTRE:[z] and as it was the

[y] Lib. xi. v. 497 : Cowper, v. 603.

Here it becomes necessary to remark, that some contradiction would seem to arise, unless the reader is reminded, that when this is first said of Hector, he was pursuing the Greeks along the *left,* or western bank of the *Scamander,* towards their rampart, after their defeat, in the *second* battle: and *before* the attack on the rampart: otherwise, when it is said that " Hector, fighting on the *left,* had " no knowledge of the valorous acts then performing by Ajax," it might have been supposed, that Hector was at that time, *opposite to the post of Ajax within the rampart,* and yet was ignorant of what was passing there. But this warfare was whilst Ajax was *in the field ;* and *before* the attack of the wall.

However, a serious difficulty occurs in lib. xiii. *v.* 675 : Cowper, v. 804; where, *within* the rampart, Hector is said not to have known yet, that, " on the " *left* of the ships, his Trojans were suffering so much: for he still kept the " position, where he first penetrated the camp, in the quarter where the ships " of Ajax and Protesilaus were."

M. Heyne, it appears, felt the same difficulty. Hector, however, might have been on the left, in a *general* sense, though not on the *flank,* or *extremity.*

[z] Iliad, lib. viii. v. 222: Cowper, v. 256. Also lib. xi. at the beginning.

The stations of Ajax and Achilles are positively spoken of : but it is only said of Agamemnon, that he ascended the ship of Ulysses, which was placed in the centre. It may however be inferred that he was then near his own station.

N

station of the Ajaces that was attacked by Hector, there is no mistaking it.[a]

In effect, then, throughout the whole attack of the rampart, in Books xii. to xvi. both inclusive, the LEFT of the GREEKS is constantly intended. And probability goes with this supposition: Achilles was sullenly neutral, and the Trojans must have wished to keep him so; and therefore would naturally avoid his station; which the ancients universally have fixed at *Sigæum;* as that of Ajax, at *Rhœteum.* It may be added, that Homer was evidently partial to the cause of the Greeks (a disposition, of which his Readers naturally partake); and that his mind, on this occasion, may be said to have resided in the camp of the Greeks.

The night adventure of Ulysses and Diomed, with Dolon the Spy, also seems to shew that Hector was on the side of *Rhœteum.*

Each party set out from his own head quarters, to proceed towards that of his enemy.[b] Consequently both proceeded on *the same line,* from opposite points: and Dolon was intercepted, at no great distance from the head quarters of the Greeks.[c] Thus far, the description suits *either extremity* of the Trojan line. But the information collected from Dolon, determined them to seek the Thracian auxiliaries,[d] who were said to be encamped in the quarter of *Thymbra.* There Ulysses and Diomed arrived, after passing through " *the bloody field strewed with arms :*"[e] which, of course, marks the

[a] Iliad, lib. xi. v. 497. Cowper, v. 603. And lib. xiii. v. 190: Cowper, v. 227.
[b] Iliad, lib. x. v. 298, 326, and 415: Cowper, v. 343, 375, and 473.
[c] v. 350, and 561: Cowper, v. 404, 646.   [d] v. 435: Cowper, 497.
[e] v. 470: Cowper, 540.

scene of the recent attacks made by Hector, to have been on the side towards *Thymbra :* or, in other words, *towards Rhœteum.*

Again, if it be admitted that the Grecian chiefs returned from the quarter of *Thymbra,* to the place from whence they first set out, *by the direct road,* (and nothing can be understood to the contrary), it would prove that Dolon came from the same quarter; since they took up his *spoils* by the way: they having been left in a marked spot.[f]

If the Reader admits the above application of the term LEFT, it could not have been otherwise, than that the *Scamander,* at that day, discharged itself into the sea, in the quarter of *Rhœteum.* And moreover, it had not varied its course considerably to the time of Demetrius : for the place of conflux of the two rivers, being then near *New Ilium,*[g] the confluent river must necessarily have ran in the line TOWARDS *Rhœteum.* (See the Map, N°. I. and N°. II.

To this may be added, that the events of the war, prove that the *Scamander* flowed *between* the Grecian camp and Troy ; as when Achilles drove the fugitive Trojans into it, in their retreat towards Troy :[h] and when Priam crossed it, not far from the Monument of Ilus, in his way to, and from the Grecian camp.[j] It is therefore impossible that the Bou_narbashi River could be the *Scamander* of Homer, let Troy be where it might : because the course of it does not intervene between Troy and the Grecian camp. And this seems to prove an oversight in M. de Chevalier.

[f] Iliad, lib. x. v. 465, and 532 ; Cowper, v. 535, 607.

[g] See above, pages 28 and 42.   [h] Iliad, lib. xxi. at the beginning.

[j] Lib. xxiv. v. 349, and 693 : Cowper, v. 439, and 367.

The Port of the *Achæans* (i. e. of the Grecians) was 12 stadia from New Ilium, in the time of Demetrius. (Strabo, pages 595, and 598.) From the form, and also from the relative position of the coast of the Hellespont, to that place ; the Port itself being also at the nearest point of the coast, to New Ilium, at that period ; it follows, that the Port of the Achæans must have been situated very far over towards *Rhœteum*. (See the Map, N°. I: and II.)

Strabo (on the authority of Demetrius we apprehend) distinguishes from the Port of the *Achæans*, the place of the *Naustathmus ;* by placing the former at 12, the latter at 20, stadia, from New Ilium : (p. 598): although they have per-haps, been often confounded together. It becomes neces-sary to distinguish them, in order to a right understanding of the position of the mouth of the *Scamander*, at different periods. He observes (p. 598), that this river discharges itself, near the *Naustathmus*, at 20 stadia from *New Ilium*, and TOWARDS, or NEAR, *Sigæum*   Also that the two rivers *Scamander* and *Simoïs*, having joined their streams in the Plain, near New Ilium, form various lakes and marshes ; and in particular, one named *Stoma-limne ;* which commu-nicated with the sea, by a *blind* mouth : that is, a channel nearly choked up with mud and sand. (Pages 595 and 597).[k] In 597, he says, that the Scamander enters the sea AT *Sigæum :* meaning, of course, at the eastern flank of its

---

[k] Hence, it may be concluded that the *Stoma-limne* was distinct from the *Naustathmus,* although near to it.

The Author has not attempted to describe the *Stoma-limne,* and other lakes and channels on the Map ; as it would have produced confusion, instead of information.

promontory; which is, however, 28 stadia distant from New Ilium, on the Map. The 20 stades fall about midway between the high land of *Sigæum* and that of *Rhæteum ;* which therefore ought to be the position of the *Naustathmus,* according to the distance given by Strabo himself. And as he has said in page 598, that the discharge was only *towards* or *near Sigæum :* thus qualifying the other assertion ; it may perhaps be concluded that he meant to say, that the mouth of the Scamander was more towards *Sigæum* than *Rhæteum.*

Pliny says (in his own time, we are left to suppose), that the joint waters of the *Xanthus* and *Simoïs,* flowed into the *Port of the Achæans ;* first forming a lake or stagnant pool, named *Palæ* (or the OLD) SCAMANDER. And that, *beyond* this Port or Inlet of the Achæans, was the *shore* of *Rhæteum.* He adds that " at a Roman mile and half from New Ilium, " was the Town and Port of *Scamandria :*" thence implied to be situated at, or near the mouth of the *Palæ Scamander.*[1] (lib. v. c. 30.)

---

[1] In describing the sea coast of the Troad, after mentioning *Alexandria Troas,* Pliny comes to " the town of *Nee ;*" then to the " *Scamander,* a *navigable* River ;" thence to *Sigæum,* a Town and Promontory ;" and finally to " the *Achæan* Port, into which flowed the collective waters of the *Xanthus* and *Simoïs.*"

The Town of *Nea-Chore,* nearly contiguous to *Jenikui,* is still found on the coast of the Ægean Sea ; between the *present* mouth of the Bounarbashi River and *Sigæum.* The former of the names, is doubtless the Greek, the latter the Turkish designation ; (for most of the places in this quarter retain their ancient Greek names) : and the meaning of both is the same : that is, *New Town.*

If this place be the *Nee* of Pliny (as we conceive it is), and the other places are to be taken, geographically, in the order in which he mentions them, then his *Navigable River* would not be the *present* Bounarbashi, as this opens to

Thus we have abundant proof, either from Strabo, or Pliny, or both, that the *Achæan* Port was 12 stadia, or about a Roman mile and half from *New Ilium;* that it was also the nearest point of the shore to that place, in or about their times ; and that it lay towards, or near *Rhæteum.* This port, therefore, answers to that of the *Æantéum;* situated at the side of the *Rhætean* Promontory, and near the Tumulus of Ajax : and which is at present named *In-Tepé-Azmah;* or the Port of the *single* Tumulus.[m] Not that the present Port, is that which existed at the date of Demetrius's or of Pliny's writing ; and much less, that of the time of the invaders, from whom it was named ; since the ground itself that surrounds it, must have been formed posterior to either : but the inlet may have been kept open, in the same line of direction, by the *back water* that continued to flow through it. And it appears incontestible, that the waters have flowed longer on this side, than on the other, by the greater increase of the alluvion, at the borders ; and the greater depth of the channel ; for this Port of the *Æantéum*, or of the *Achæans,* continued to the time of Constantine, to receive fleets. (Chandler's Hist. Troy, p. 152.)

It is in the neighbourhood of the *Achæan* Port, that the

the sea, southward of *Nea-chore;* and not between it and *Sigæum.* But to the Author it appears the most probable, that the names *Scamander* and *Sigæum,* are transposed in Pliny.

[m] It appears that the Turks distinguish the Tumulus ascribed to Ajax, by the name of *In Tepe;* i. e. the *single,* or one *Mount* : and those of Achilles and Patroclus, by *Duo* or *Dio;* the *two Mounts.* Of course, the Turks, on their first establishment in Asia Minor, received these names from the Greeks. M. de Chevalier has made the latter name, *Dios;* and applied it to the Tumulus of Achilles, *alone.* (Francklin).

site of *Scamandria* is to be looked for : that is, at the mouth of the OLD *Scamander*, which *had flowed*, but which had long *ceased to flow*, into the *Achæan* Port, as a regular stream. Nor can it well be doubted, that *Scamandria* derived its name from the river which ran by it. It is mentioned only by Pliny (it would appear) : and it is probable that its Port became the Port of *New Ilium*.

Thus the position of the *Achæan Port*, appears clear and satisfactory : as also that the *Scamander* and its adjuncts, *once* fell into it.

Although the place of discharge of the *Scamander* is given differently by Demetrius and Pliny, yet on examination, perhaps the accounts may not be found, on the whole, irreconcileable. The Scamander spoken of by the former, was doubtless that of *his own time ;* but the PALÆ *Scamander* of the latter, by the name, may have been that of remote times. It is also proper to observe, that the *Achæan Port*, and the *Naustathmus*, could not, from the nature of the place, be more than a mile distant from each other ; and perhaps less : and it will appear, from what has been quoted above, that the waters connected with them formed extensive lakes ; particularly that, which communicated with the *Naustathmus* (Strabo, page 595.) Is it then too much to suppose, that *two sets* of lakes, so near each other, should communicate by lateral channels ; and the rivers themselves, by the medium of these ; especially as they owed their formation to the same river, at different periods ? This may serve to explain the meaning of Pliny, without violence to that of Strabo ; or rather of Demetrius.[n]

With respect to the *Scamander amnis navigabilis* of Pliny, (See note to

On the whole, then, we trust that it will appear as clear to the Reader, as it does to the Author, that the *Scamander* formerly ran by *Rhœteum ;* where the memory of the fact appears to have been preserved in the very name of the river.° Also that the mouth of the river has varied in its course, between the two Promontories : that it had gone somewhat more than half way over, towards the *Sigœan* side, in the time of Demetrius : and is at present, *at* that side.

The Karanlik Inlet, the *head* of which appears to answer to the position of the *Naustathmus* of Strabo, is now in the state in which he describes the mouth of the *Stoma-limne* to have been ; that is, shut up by a bank of mud and sand.ᴾ But here, as well as at the site of the *Achœan* Port, the ground has all grown up, since the time of Strabo : although an *opening* may have continued in the same direction at the latter place, from the discharge of land-floods : and indeed the In-Tepe-Azmah seems to be the *opening* of the *Old Scamander ;* as the Karanlik, of a *more recent one.*

The *Thymbrius* River, according to Strabo, (p. 598), was intercepted in its way to the Sea by the *Scamander :* as it was also, perhaps, at the date of the *Achœan* invasion : but

page 93), it appears on every account irreconcileable, that a *navigable Scamander* should have flowed into the *Ægean* Sea, whilst at the same time the confluent waters of the *Xanthus* and *Simoïs,* (that is the *Scamander* and *Simoïs*) are described by the same author, to flow into the bay between *Sigœum* and *Rhœteum !*

° Nothing is more common in tropical climates, where rivers often change their courses, than to have *duplicates* of the same name : that is, of the *existing* river ; and of the *old,* or former river ; in many instances of which, the *bed,* with *stagnant pools* only, remains, except at its *embouchure.*

ᴾ *Karanlik* is said to mean, in the Turkish language, the *closed port.*

that of Bounarbashi might at the same time have gained the sea, on the side of *Sigæum*, by a separate channel from the Mender. If the Shimar (*Simoïs*) had, at that time, distinct summer and winter courses, as at present, they might have ran much in the same lines of direction also; and its conflux with the Mender, in the time of Demetrius, might have been effected by the means of a slight variation of its *present* summer course, along the front of New Ilium; the Mender (*Scamander*) falling into it, at a point between Kalifatli and Koumkui.

It may be proper to remark, that although the distinction of *winter* course is given, because it is *more frequently swoln,* at that season, than at others; yet that it may be supposed to join at Kalifatli, *at any season,* when in a *swoln* state. See above, page 43.

To conclude the present article, it may be said, that no other line of direction of the *Scamander*, than that towards *Rhœteum,* can be conceived to have taken place, in the time ef Homer, consistently with the transactions recorded in the Iliad; since it intervened between the Greek camp and Troy: and admitting that course, all appears consistent, in respect of the present article. Experience so fully proves the wandering of rivers, through their own alluvions, that it is unnecessary to dwell on the subject in this place. And Mr. Gell actually describes a number of *deserted* channels of rivers, and beds of lakes in the quarter just spoken of; the former of which pointed towards *Rhœteum* (Troy, page 40). And he expresses his opinion, that such must have been the ancient course of the river.

Mr. Gell also (page 42) quotes Sophocles (in Ajax) as mani-

o

festing a belief that the *Scamander* ran near the quarter of Ajax—and indeed the exclamation of that hero, " O ! neigh-" bouring streams of *Scamander*, kindly propitious to the " Greeks ! ⁹" does certainly lead to a conclusion, that Sophocles, either from a careful examination of the story of the Iliad, or from a received tradition, believed that the *Scamander* ran by the quarter of Ajax ; that is, of course, by the *left*, or eastern side of the Grecian fortification.

⁹ Dr. Gillies.

SECTION V.

THE THROSMOS, OR RISE OF THE PLAIN, ABOVE THE SEA BEACH.

The term Throsmos *differently understood—appears to mean the* ascent *from the Sea Beach, to the* Plain.—*Position of the Trojan Line on the* Throsmos; *and extending thence, into the Valley of* Thymbra.

THE Trojans, after the second battle (lib. viii. v. 213,)[r] having driven the Greeks from the Plain before Troy, and compelled them to take shelter behind their wall; meditated an attack on that, and on the fleet, the next morning; and for this purpose, they took post so near, as to be *within hearing* of the Grecian camp: of course, it may be concluded, that it was within the distance of five or six hundred yards. And, in this position, they were said to be encamped on the THROSMOS;[s] understood to mean the rise of the Plain, or the *step up* from the sea beach, to the country within: as they were also said to have been " *beside the ships.*"[t]

[r] Cowper, v. 242.

[s] —— " *opposite*, on the *rising ground*, appear'd
The Trojans." Lib. xi. v. 56: Cowper, v. 68.
And this is repeated, in xx. v. 3: Cowper, v. 3.

[t] Lib. x. v. 160.
—— " on the *rising ground* beside the ships,
Our num'rous foes still menace us." Cowper, v. 188.

There are different opinions amongst the learned, respecting the precise meaning of the term THROSMOS, as applied on this occasion.[u] Some have supposed it to mean *a lofty mound*, rising from the midst of the Plain; whilst Mr. Gell takes it for the *heights* of *Sigæum*; which extend along the coast of the *Ægean* Sea. As the Trojans, calculated at 50,000, were encamped ON the THROSMOS, the former opinion, consequently, must be erroneous; and Mr. Gell's right, as to *the nature of the thing*. But the heights of *Sigæum* seem, from their *position*, to be ill adapted to the service of blockading and watching the Greeks, for the purposes intended : because they were not only *too remote* from, but also *oblique* to, the position of the Greek line; being nearly parallel to the course of the Mender.

The *Throsmos* must surely mean the *first rising*, or *step*, of the ground, from the beach of the sea; which appears to have been *shelving*, by what is said concerning the disposition of the rows of ships : [x]and the edge of the Plain beyond it, would be to the Greeks on the beach, *a rising ground*.

---

[u] The word THROSMOS is well known to be derived from *Throsko, to leap*, or *leap up*. (Dr. Gillies.) It appears to mean an elevated spot of any kind above the general level; short of what may properly be termed *a hill*. In effect, a *rising ground*: and in the present case, may mean the *step up*, or *sudden rise* of the Plain, above the sea beach.

Mr. Heyne was very near it, when he said, " The Trojans had taken post on " the field of battle, which had an *acclivity towards Troy*." (Edinburgh Trans. Vol. iv. p. 105.

[x] " *Line above line ascending*." (Lib. xiv. v. 35 : Cowper, v. 41.)
And

——————— " the barks which landing first
Were station'd *highest* on the *shelving* shore."—
(Lib. xv. v. 653 : Cowper, v. 770.)

And as it must have been of course, parallel to the shore of the Bay, it would afford a very proper position for an army employed in watching another, in such a position, with a view to an almost immediate attack. Nor does Mr. Gell's expression of " *dead flat*," on which the village and Tumulus of Koum-kui are said to stand,[y] at all combat this idea : for the first *rise*, or *step*, up from the beach, was undoubtedly between the *Tumulus* of Koum-kui and the margin of the sea. But even had the ground been perfectly flat, throughout, the *position* in question, would have been the fittest for the purpose of the Trojans.

It appears then, that the position of the Trojan line of encampment on the *Throsmos*, was within hearing of the Grecian camp :[z] also, that the same line must have approached very near to the Tomb of Ilus :[a] which Tomb was also close to the bank of the Scamander.[b] Moreover, that the Trojan camp, which thus occupied the *Throsmos*, lay between the Grecian wall, and the Scamander.[c] That Hector's attack was on the *left* of the Grecian camp, and also *by* the Scamander ;[d] which river must therefore have ran on the left, (or to the eastward) of the Greeks. And as they would scarcely have taken a *torrent bed* of that magnitude and description, *into* their camp, it may reasonably be inferred, that they covered their left flank with it. (See again the

[y] See above, page 83.

[z] Iliad, lib. x. v. 14: Cowper, v. 13.

Agamemnon " heard pipes, and recorders, and the hum of war."

[a] Lib. viii. v. 490: Cowper, 563. And lib. x. v. 415 : Cowper, 473.

[b] See above, page 88.   [c] Lib. viii. v. 556 : Cowper, v. 644.

[d] See above, page 87, *et seq.*

Map, N°. II.) And, on the other hand, it is equally probable, that the Trojans, on the like principle, would not have taken their position, in such a way, as to allow the river to *divide* their *national* army ;ᵉ or even to separate any part of it, from an enemy whom they meant to attack at day-break. And this would agree with the text; which says, that " the " Trojan camp lay between the Grecian wall and the *Sca-mander*." It may therefore be concluded that the right flank of the *national army* of Troy, was also covered by the left bank of the *Scamander;* having the *ford*, and the Tomb of *Ilus* in the rear of the camp: but possibly, little farther distant from it, than the breadth of the river bed.

If then it be admitted, that the *Tumulus* at Koum-kui answers to that of Ilus, the Trojan line on the *Throsmos* may be supposed to have ranged below it; with the auxiliaries extending on a continuation of the same line, eastward, into the Valley of *Thymbra;* and thence to the margin of the sea, within *Rhœteum;* the Bay, at that time, it may be supposed, approaching, or even entering the mouth of the valley. That the auxiliaries were there posted, is learnt from the report of Dolon; who places the *Mœonians*, *Phrygians*, and *Lycians*, there; and the *Carians*, by the sea-side.ᶠ And it may be conceived that, on the other hand, the Trojan line extended westward, to the foot of the high land of *Sigœum*: thus embracing the whole *front* of the Greeks, as well as their *flanks*.

ᵉ Used in contradistinction to the auxiliaries; who, according to Dolon, occupied the Valley of *Thymbra*, &c. and consequently, were beyond the *Scamander*.

ᶠ Iliad, lib. x. v. 426: Cowper, v. 488.

We are concerned thus to differ from some of our friends, who have fixed the Trojan encampment, along the high land of *Sigæum;* which they regard as the *Throsmos* of Homer. But it is to be considered, what the object of the Trojans was, in taking a position on the *Throsmos.* They had driven their enemy off the field, and cooped him up, in his defective intrenchments : and were only waiting the return of day, to storm them, and destroy the fleet within. They were, moreover, watching the motions of the Greeks ; that they might be enabled to fall suddenly upon them, if they attempted to launch their vessels ; for such was the declared purpose of Hector,[g] (and which gave rise to the fears of Ulysses, expressed to Agamemnon) ;[h] consequently, it was necessary, that the Trojans should take a position very near. Now, the high land of *Sigæum* (Jenishehr) not only extended in a direction, which was by no means parallel to the front of the Greeks ; but also *lay far beyond their right :* and must have been from a mile, to a mile and quarter distant from the wall. It was therefore ill suited to the purposes, either of watching them, or of attacking them suddenly. But the rise of the Plain, in front, (or the *step up* from the

[g] Lib. viii. v. 510.
 " Illume the skies; lest even in the night,
 Launching, they mount the billows, and escape." (Cowper, v. 585.)
And, v. 530.
 ———— " arming with the morrow, at their ships
 Give them brisk onset." (Cowper, v. 609.)
[h] Lib. xiv. v. 100.
 ———— " For while they draw
 Their gallies seaward, thither will they look,
 Nor check the foe, nor heed the battle more." (Cowper, v. 114.)

beach), afforded a *parallel position;* which was the most proper, and advantageous, in every point of view.

It may also be said, that the Greeks were *closely pursued* to their wall, before the Trojans formed their camp : also that it is repeatedly said, that the latter were encamped *opposite to the wall :* and finally, that after the defeat of the Trojans in the third battle, which was fought *on the Throsmos ;* they were pursued from thence, " *through the middle of the Plain,* " *beside the Sepulchre of Ilus,*"ⁱ &c. seeking to regain the town.

Thus much may be said for the *probability* of what we have contended for. Nor would the position of *Sigæum* agree with the *history :* for the Trojan camp lay " *between* the *wall* and the *Scamander ;*" and also " *near the ships.*" This cannot be reconciled to a position, along the high land of *Sigæum* let the course of the Scamander be where it might : not to mention, that the term *Throsmos* means, if we are rightly informed, a LEAP; or perhaps here, a STEP up, from the beach: not a *hill.*

ⁱ Probably, because the fords of the river were in that quarter: as appears by the journey of Priam, lib. xxiv, v. 349, and 693 : Cowper, v. 439, and 867. And also, by the circumstance of Hector being carried thither, in lib. xiv, v. 434. (See note to page 59.)

SECTION III.

CONCERNING THE TUMULUS OF ÆSYETES.

Udjek-Tepe *or* Tumulus, *entirely out of the question, as being too far* distant, *and* not within the Plain; *as Demetrius describes that of Æsyetes to be—Supposed to be that, at the former conflux of the Mender and Bounarbashi Rivers—Two* Tumuli *recently discovered by* Dr. Clarke.

N̲o *Tumulus* is found in the position assigned by Demetrius (Strabo, p. 599), at 5 stadia from *New Ilium,* on the road to *Alexandria Troas.*[k]

It appears evident, from the story, that, wheresoever Polites stood, to reconnoitre the Grecian army, he must have been exposed to the hazard of being cut off from Troy by the Greeks; otherwise, he could not be said to have trusted to his " *superior speed* " for his escape.[l] This then, bespeaks a situation, *at least* as far from Troy, as was the Grecian camp: which description, combined with the circumstance of *a proper distance for viewing his object* (a particular that does not seem to have been attended to, by some of the commentators), appears to us, to be applicable to no other *known Tumulus,* than that, at the ancient conflux of

---

[k] This was written, previous to the publication of Dr. Clarke's second volume.

[l] It is said, Iliad, lib. ii. v. 791, *et seq.* that " Priam's son, Polites, who, trusting to his swiftness of foot, sat as *scout* for the Trojans, on the top of the Tomb of Old Æsyetes; watching when the Greeks would *advance to battle from their ships.*"

the Mender and Bounarbashi Rivers: [m] the *Ilus* monument of Mr. Gell.   But this is from 15 to 18 stadia, instead of 5, from New Ilium; and does not lie in the direct road to *Alexandria Troas*.

It appears altogether extraordinary that Udjek Tepe should ever have been fixed on, for the Tumulus of Æsyetes. It is from 5 to 6 miles from the site of the Grecian camp. What could be seen from thence; and before the invention of telescopes? And had Troy been at Bounarbashi, as this system supposes, the person employed to reconnoitre had 3 miles less to run, than his pursuers.   A man could not be said to be in danger of being overtaken, who had the start of his pursuers by 2 or 3 miles: and had not more than twice that distance to run.

It may be added, that, although an army might have been visible from Udjek Tepe, yet that a single individual was too small an object to be seen from the army.

The ideas of Demetrius were very different.   He speaks of the *Tumulus* of Æsyetes, as being, in common with those of Ilus, and Myrinna, situated WITHIN the PLAIN OF TROY (Strabo, page 597): whereas Udjek Tepe is on the HILLS that shut up the Plain on the south: which is, surely, as different from the text of Strabo, as its position is in every respect improbable.

The Tumulus at the former conflux of the Mender and Bounarbashi Rivers, may have been about a mile and quarter from the Grecian wall: which was not an inconvenient distance, from whence to observe, with the *naked eye*,

---

[m] That is, the place where the conflux *was*, before the turning of the Bounarbashi River from its former course, into the *Ægean* Sea.

the order and motions of a line of troops: For, one of the objects may probably have been, to ascertain whether or not, Achilles marched with the army to the first battle ; a matter of great importance to the Trojans, to know.

One does not comprehend why there should have been a necessity for Polites to expose either his person, or the knowledge of his being present, if the object was completed by a personal communication of his intelligence. It is therefore to be suspected, that the person employed to reconnoitre, was in the first instance, *to make signals*, either to the Citadel of Troy, *direct ;* or to some point, from whence they were *repeated* to Troy.

It may not be improper to observe, that the position of the Tumulus at the conflux, is such, as to command a *full view* of the coast of the Bay of the Mender: so that the Grecian line would have been *open to the view*, throughout its whole extent. (See N°. II.)

*** Of the two *Tumuli* seen by Dr. Clarke, one, as we have remarked (page 86), commands a view of the Bay of the *Scamander.* Not only the objection stated, against the probability of Udjek being the *Tumulus* of *Æsyetes*, holds in this case ; (viz.) that no hazard could be incurred, by reason of its being so much nearer to Troy ; but the line of view from it, would have been nearly that of the direction of the Grecian line of battle : so that the *parts* of that line, could not be *separated*, by reason of the *fore-shortening.*

It must however be admitted, that the *Tumulus* seen by Dr. Clarke, appears to agree nearly with Strabo's distance from New Ilium. But it is worthy of remark, that the Monument of Æsyetes is never mentioned, but on occasion of Polites' exploring the Grecian camp ; and therefore cannot be supposed to have lain in the way of the armies, during their warfare ; as that seen by Dr. Clarke certainly may. (See the Maps, Nº. I. and II.)

PART III.

CONCERNING WHAT MAY BE COLLECTED FROM THE
ANCIENTS, POSTERIOR TO THE TIME OF HOMER,
RESPECTING THE SITE OF TROY, THE FIELDS
OF BATTLE, &c.

PART III.

SECTION I.

The Pagus Iliensium *supposed by Demetrius to have stood on
a part of the* ANCIENT TROY *or* ILIUM—*Placed on his
Authority—The Tumulus taken for that of* Myrinna, *accords
with this System—*Troy, (*the* Pergama *excepted*) *said to have
been situated in a Plain—Temples of Apollo, in the Valley of*
Thymbra—*One of them lately discovered by Messrs.* Francklin
and Hope—Bounarbashi *too far distant from the Sea, to
answer to* Troy ;—*which is proved to have been much nearer,
by the Events of the* third *Battle : as also, by certain Transactions of the Trojans, whilst encamped on the* Throsmos.

IT has been stated, that the Ancients, even before the time
of the Augustan age, did not pretend to fix the *exact site* of
Troy: but only pointed out that of the *Pagus Iliensium ;*
which Demetrius says,[n] was *thought* to stand on a part of
the site of Ancient Troy: in other words, that a *village*
stood on a part of the same ground, which the *City of the
same name* formerly occupied ; the like of which has happened in other places. But in the recital of Demetrius,

[n] Strabo, pages 593, 597

there are certain particulars, which seem to shew that the *general site* must have been known. "We are shewn," says he, "the *Erineus*, *Myrinna*, and Barrow of *Ilus*." Now the *Erineus* is known to have *adjoined* to the walls:[o] and the Tomb of *Myrinna* stood before, and at no great distance from the *Scæan* Gate.[p]

New Ilium, or the Ilium of the days of Demetrius, and of Strabo, has been already placed (page 41) on a hill about a mile to the S. E. of Koum-kui; and on the south side of the entrance of the Valley of Thymbrek, or *Thymbra*.

The *Pagus Iliensium* was 30 stadia higher up the country, towards the *east*, and *Mount Ida;* (Strabo, p. 593); 10 short of the *Kalli-colone*, or *beautiful hill*, said to be near the *Simoïs:* and to which, the hill of Atchekui (with the exception of its being rather too far from the river[q]), appears to answer, in position and description. For it being a little short of $4\frac{3}{4}$ British miles from that side of New Ilium, towards the mouth of the Mender, the distance may be taken at 47 to 48 stades of the scale of Strabo: and allowing 7 or 8 for the extent of New Ilium, eastward; the 40 stades given between that *City* and the *Kalli-colone*, will be made out.

Forty stades are *also* given, in *one line of distance*, between

[o] Iliad, lib. vi. v. 433: Cowper, v. 486.

One must conceive the *Erineus* to have been a rising ground, or swell, which adjoined in one part of its extent, to the city wall; and rendered the access to it less difficult. Some beech trees growing on it, appear to have given it the name. It seems to have extended to some distance from Troy; as it was passed in the way from the Grecian camp to the *Scæan* Gate. It may have been a continuation of the swell described in page 39.

[p] Iliad, lib. iii. v. 144: Cowper, v. 179.

[q] See above, page 46.

New Ilium and the *Kalli-colone*, in Strabo, page 598; confirming the other statement of 30 and 10, in *two* lines. So that *New Ilium*, the *Pagus Iliensium*, and the *Kalli-colone*, should all three have lain nearly in a direct line; and that line pointing *eastward* from New Ilium; or towards *Ida.*[r]

It is not, however, pretended, that the *site* of the *Pagus Iliensium* can be ascertained. It may be sufficient to the purpose, that the distance between New Ilium and Atchekui, the supposed *Kalli-colone*, agrees in the gross: and then to consider the general site of the *Pagus*, as being about ten stadia from Atchekui, in the direction of *New Ilium*.

Mr. Gell, in his Book, page 90, and View, N°. xxxiii, from Bounarbashi, points out a hill, which accords with the supposed situation of the *Pagus*: it is seen at the left extremity of the plate; and in the back ground. The hill itself appears in the view, to be such a one, as might have borne on its summit, a Citadel or *Pergama*; such as is described to have been in, or adjacent to, Ancient Troy: and indeed, it appears probable, that the *Ilieans* would have secured to themselves the possession of the site of the *Pergama*, as a post, strong by its natural defences.

The hill in question is placed on the Map, N°. I., by the process described in the note, at the foot of the page.[s] And

---

[r] By the Topography, one must consider it to be more *south-eastward* than *eastward.* These niceties are often disregarded in modern, as well as in ancient descriptions. *Winter-east* is a term sometimes employed by the Ancients: and would suit the present case.

[s] From the *Tumulus* over Bounarbashi, the angle was measured between Atchekui, and the hill in question: and this was intersected by a *cross bearing*

in this position, its base may approach within 10 or 12 stades of that of the hill of Atchekui :[t] and may be five, or less, from the River Shimar, the supposed *Simoïs*.

The distance from the foot of the supposed hill of the *Pagus*, to the *Tumulus* in the Plain, taken by Mr. Gell, for that of *Myrinna*,[u] is about a mile and half : and to the bank of the Mender may be somewhat more. So that, admitting the *Pergama* of Troy, to have been situated on the hill, in question ; the *City* may well have extended from the foot of that hill, across the Plain, to the neighbourhood of the Mender (*Scamander*): having, in that case, the just mentioned *Tumulus* lying before it ; as the Poet says of that of Myrinna ; where Hector drew up his army, previous to the first battle, in the second Book of the Iliad :[x] according to which sup-

from Kalifatli. Both of these were measured on Mr. Gell's Map, No. XLV, with the aid also of the View, N°. xxxiii.

First, however, the bearing of Atchekui was corrected, in a small degree, by a line from the before-mentioned Tumulus to the Asian Castle (of *Abydus*) : for all the three appear to lie very nearly in one line, of N°. $13\frac{1}{4}$ E : Mr. Gell's being a trifle different ; or N. 16 E.

[t] The distance of Atchekui from Bounarbashi has also undergone some correction ; by which it is placed somewhat farther off, than Mr. Gell allows ; but which agrees better with M. Kauffer. The correction is founded on Mr. Carlyle's proportion of the time, employed between Thymbrek-kui and Bounarbashi, which was $2\frac{1}{4}$ hours. Out of this interval, 65. min. were employed between Atchekui and Bounarbashi ; equal to $2\frac{1}{4}$ miles of Mr. Gell's scale (which has been followed, in the gross). This correction is borne out by the calculation of Captain Francklin.

[u] See above, page 40.

[x] The people of Kalifatli, a village situated within a mile and half of this *Tumulus*, have an idea that their village stands *on a part of the site of Ancient Troy*. (Gell's Troy, page 57.)

position, the City of Troy would have occupied the middle space between the *Simoïs* and the *Scamander;* and approached within half a mile of either.

That the City, at large, stood in a Plain, we are told by Homer (Iliad xx. v. 215): Æneas, speaking of times, previous to its foundation, says, " Ilium had not yet been reared, in the *Plain.*" ʸ Strabo speaks to the same effect, in pages 592, and 593. But if the ground at Bounarbashi be examined, it will be found, that the *whole* site of the supposed Troy of M. Chevalier, is *hilly*, for nearly a mile and half from the *Pergama*, to the place of *his Scæan* Gate. Nor can a *Kalli-colone* be found at 10 stadia from it, in the quarter opposite to New Ilium; as the description requires.

Dr. Dallaway saw on a hill, at the distance of an hour and half of travelling, short of Bounarbashi Hill, some columns of a *very ancient* form. The position answers to that of the ruins of a temple marked by M. Kauffer, at about a mile and half to the S. E.-ward of Chiblak; on the edge of the great Plain of the Mender, and very close to the hill of the *supposed Pergama.*

The hill of Atchekui, if allowed to be the *Kalli-colone;* as Dr. Chandler, Mr. Gell, and M. de Chevalier suppose,

---

ʸ Homer says, " He (Dardanus) built *Dardania :* for SACRED ILIUM had not yet been reared, in the Plain; the city of *many-languaged* men." *Ilium* should seem to have been one of those sacred *emporia,* where men speaking different languages, traded safely under the protection of temples. (Dr. Gillies.)

₊ The Author begs leave to refer the Reader to Dr. Gillies's History of the World, from the reign of Alexander to that of Augustus, Vol. I. page 68, *et seq.* where the subject of this highly ancient commerce is treated at large.

and as appearances seem to warrant ; (see above, page 45) affords no contemptible evidence, towards a proof that the *Pagus Iliensium* stood where Mr. Gell supposes; and that the Tumulus below it, stood in the Plain of Troy ; and was the *Myrinna,* or *Batiæa.* Both the beautiful hill and the *Tumulus,* to agree with the history, must have stood between the *Scamander* and *Simoïs.*[z]

The Valley of *Thymbra* is said by Strabo, (p. 598) to have been near Troy. This, however, can only be meant *generally.* The supposed Hill of the *Pagus* is more than two miles from the Valley of Thymbrek (i. e. *Thymbra*) ; but certainly about twice that distance from the supposed *Pergama,* over Bounarbashi.

Strabo also says, in the same page, that the Temple of Apollo *Thymbræus* was 50 stadia from *New Ilium.* The ruins of a great and magnificent temple, are found near Kalil-Eli; and are universally thought to be those of the temple in question : but they are not more than 10 stadia from the nearest part of the site of New Ilium.

Capt. Francklin and Mr. Philip Hope, after visiting these ruins, saw the ruins of another temple, at 4 miles higher up the Valley of Thymbrek : and at one mile beyond, (or to the Eastward of) Thymbrek-kui, or the Village of Thymbrek. Captain F. says, that it was situated in a grove of stately firs : and " was formerly a temple of superb and " beautiful architecture of the *Doric* order ; which appears " from the numerous fragments of columns, capitals, and

---

[z] Messrs. Hope and Francklin saw, at Atchekui, two columns of " *gray granite, of an order unknown,* and *very ancient.*"

" pedestals of the finest Parian marble. It is called by the
" natives, *Thymbrek Muzarlik;* or Cemetery of Thymbrek."
(Francklin's Tour, pages 11 and 12.)

The position of this temple agrees with Strabo's distance
of 50 stadia from *New Ilium:* and it is, perhaps, the very
temple intended by him. The other may have been built
posterior to the time of Demetrius (from whose description,
Strabo probably spoke; as in most other places); and during
the season, when the Romans were so besotted with their
supposed Trojan origin. It would be worth the attention of
future travellers, to examine the style of the two masses of
ruins; with a view to ascertain their antiquity; and whether
the most retired, is not the most ancient of the two:

Captain Francklin says, that most of the columns at Kalil-
Eli, were *Corinthian,* (pages 8 and 9): but M. de Chevalier
says, *Doric;* with *scattered* capitals of *Corinthian.* Who shall
decide! The original temple, from whence Apollo derived
his name of THYMBRÆUS, must needs have been very
ancient, and before the date of the Corinthian order.[a]

To return to the subject of the position of Troy, and that
of the supposed *Pagus Iliensium.*—It may perhaps be objected, that the springs which arose before the *Scæan* Gate,
are wanting. To this it may be answered, that the ground,

[a] Dr. Clarke's account of the ruins near Kalil-Eli, (Vol. II. page 84), is sub-
joined; but it does not remove the doubt, altogether.

" The ruins we found, were rather the remains of ten temples, than of one.
" The earth, to a considerable distance, was covered by subverted and broken
" columns of marble, granite, and of every order in architecture. *Doric, Ïonic,*
" and *Corinthian* capitals, lay dispersed in all directions: and some of these
" were of great beauty."

on that side, has not been sufficiently examined, to know whether there are, or are not, any springs, in the situation alluded to: and that Strabo (page 602) speaks of *a cold* spring, which, it appears, would have answered the purpose, had there been also a *hot* one near it. And he certainly looked for Troy in this quarter. But, in a country so subject to earthquakes, springs are often destroyed in one place, and break out in another. Nothing, perhaps, is so easily destroyed by an earthquake, as the locality of a spring.

In the next place, we shall enquire, how far the distance of Troy, from the Camp of the Greeks, collected from the transactions in the Iliad, agrees with the actual topography before us. If we are to conclude, as appears reasonable, that Homer meant to represent the *bulk* of the *individuals* of the contending armies, as possessing in mind, as well as in body, no more than the ordinary powers of men; [b] it will be found, that the great excess in point of *distance*, that must have been marched over, in a given time, by the armies (if we follow M. de Chevalier's system) presents a difficulty equal to any that has yet occurred.

It ought, doubtless, to be expected, that the Poet should be as consistent in this matter, as in any other part of his subject. Had he, for instance, described such an extent of

[b] That such they were meant to be represented, appears certain, from more than one passage in the Iliad. As when (in lib. xiv. v. 100: Cowper, 114,) Ulysses expres-es his fears to Agamemnon, respecting the conduct of the troops, in the event of a precipitate retreat, from the Trojan shores. And again (in xxiv. v. 454: Cowper, v. 566), where the strength of three Grecians was required to move the bar of Achilles's tent (or rather hut) door; but which *he* was in the habit of moving by the means of his own personal strength.

ground marched over, in a given time, as is nearly double that, to which the powers of men are equal; the *military critics,* at least, would not have suffered such an inconsistency to pass: and he was doubtless aware, as we have before remarked, that the ground, and the principal positions in it, were known to the well-informed part of his readers.

Now, had one of those military critics been shewn the hills of Bounarbashi, for the site of Troy, would he not have regretted the want of judgment in the Poet, who should have admitted so glaring an inconsistency, in one of the marked features of the history of the war. For the fact is, that the *Scæan* Gate of M. de Chevalier, is full 7 British miles in a *straight* line from the site of the Grecian wall: and on the days on which Hector assaulted it, the ground in question was *four times* marched over: that is, the Grecians twice repulsed the Trojans from their wall, to Troy; and were as often beaten back. So that the ground gone over, was full 28 miles in a *right line;* and certainly 30 at the very least, if not 32: by the road.[c]

The great battle on the *Throsmos,* when the Greeks sallied from their rampart, early in the morning, was not decided

---

[c] M. de Chevalier's Map, has   -   -   7½ British miles.
   Mr. Gell's   -   -   -   -   7
   Mr. Kauffer's   -   -   -   7
         Mean, *over 7,* in a *direct line.*

Mr. Hawkins, Dr. Sibthorpe, and Captain Francklin, severally estimate the distance between the sea at Koumkala, and Bounarbashi, at 9 miles; which would give much the same result from the supposed site of the rampart. M. de Chevalier says 4 leagues. (Troy, page 116.)

till the hour of noon : ^d and the whole operations of the day, great and important as they were, ended before sunset.^e The *longest day* in that parallel has only 7½ hours of *sun*, between noon and sunset.^f This then, places the matter out of all question. For the four marches, collectively equal to 30 miles, or more, did not commence till the end of the first battle on the *Throsmos*: or at noon. Of course 7½ hours (taking the longest day) were not sufficient even for the *marching* of a great army in order of battle, 30 miles : and here, they are said, not only to have *marched*, but also to have *fought*, over a great part of the ground : and moreover, to have also fought thrice at the wall : once in *front* of it, the other times *within* it ; after it was taken by assault. Then a fresh attack was made by Patroclus, who *drove out* the Trojans : and after all, there was much fighting *before* Troy ; and also *before* the wall, for the body of Patroclus.

If, then, Homer be supposed to treat of battles, and marches, that were real subjects of history, Troy could not have been 7 miles and upwards, from the *ancient sea-coast;* as M. de Chevalier's Map requires. But if the *Pagus Iliensium* stood on a part of the site of Troy, (as Demetrius supposed) the distance might have been less than 4 miles from

^d See the woodman's time of dinner, in lib. xi. v. 87. Cowper, v. 107.

^e Lib. xviii. v. 241 : Cowper, v. 292.

Troy is said to have been taken exactly at the summer solstice. Twenty-nine days elapsed between the third battle, and the end of the truce for Hector's funeral. How long an interval might be required for the subsequent transactions, it is difficult to say ; but surely a *month* does not seem too long. This would bring the third battle to the latter end of April ; when the sun would be above the horizon about 13¼ hours ; and consequently the interval between noon and sunset, would be short of 7 hours ; or strictly, 6 h. 52 min.

the Grecian wall to the *Scæan* Gate; admitting that the City extended into the Plain, towards the Tumulus, taken by Mr. Gell for that of Myrinna.[g] Then, the whole sum of the marches, might have been no more than 15 or 16 miles; or about an ordinary day's march, for an army: so that, after allowing a reasonable time for that service, an interval might still remain for the other transactions. But these were so numerous and important, that it must still be allowed, the interval is *short:* but here, is at least, a *possibility* of doing it; which the system of M. de Chevalier does not even admit.   And, it is remarkable, that the intervals of time, on that day, are marked with unusual precision. With *the light of day*, the Greeks prepare to make the attack on the Trojans posted on the *Throsmos:* and sally forth.   At *noon*, the Trojans first give way; and *" the Greeks forc'd ev'ry phalanx of the foe."* (lib. xi. v. 90: Cowper, v. 114.) And when the *sun set*, *" the Achians ceas'd from the all-wasting labours of the war."* (lib. xviii. v. 241. Cowper, v. 292.)

It is entertaining enough to observe how easily some have got rid of the difficulty, arising from the *great excess* in the distance; by saying that the transactions required a great extent of space: but surely, the *simple movements* described

[g] Or, the distance between the Camp, and the *Pagus*, may be taken in this way. Demetrius allows 6 stadia between the sea coast and New Ilium (but which we have corrected to 8½); and 30, thence to the *Pagus Iliensium:* Total 38½ stades. To this distance is to be added, the extent of the city of New Ilium, in that direction; for which, if 8 stadia be allowed, there will be a grand total of 46½; (or nearly 4¾ British miles.) But as the *Scæan* Gate is the point reckoned to, in the former calculation, the supposed extent of Troy is to be deducted from the 46½ stades: and then, this result will be much the same as the other.

by Homer, required no more than the ordinary space which armies take to form in. Again, others reason as if large armies, in order of battle, moved with the celerity of a company of ordinary travellers.

Much stress has been laid, on the saying of Polydamus, that

"We are remote from Troy;"[h]

when they were at the Grecian wall.   But, besides that the term *remote*, is *comparative*, the same phrase is made use of by Priam to Achilles, in speaking of the Forests of Ida.— "remote from Ida:" when the distance from Troy to the mountain intended, was at most only 3 or 4 miles.

The circumstance the most in point, respecting the vicinity of Troy to the Grecian Camp, is, perhaps, that of the quick arrival of the provisions, from Troy; when Hector was encamped on the *Throsmos*, watching the Greeks, within their fortification.   Hector says to his Trojans, " Night has intervened, to which the Grecians owe their safety—Now therefore, take, as your necessities require, needful refreshment —with dispatch, drive hither from the *city* fatted sheep and oxen: fetch bread from your houses; make speedy purchase of wine; and gather plenty of fuel.[i] "

These preparations were for the *present night;* and the order was not given till *after night fall:* probably so late as 8 o'clock, as it seems to have been about the end of April; (See the note to page 120); and an attack on the Grecian Camp, intended at daybreak; perhaps before 4; or in less than $7\frac{1}{2}$ hours after the order was given.   If, then, Bounar-

---

[h] Iliad, lib. xviii. 256: Cowper, v. 310.
[i] Lib. viii. v. 497, *et seq.* Cowper, v. 573.

bashi stands on the site of Troy, fifteen miles at least (as we have shewn before), were to be gone over, out and home; in order to *collect* and *fetch* the articles of refreshment. A chief part of it consisted of sheep and oxen; some of the most *slow-paced* of animals: these were to be slaughtered, prepared, and dressed; and a needful time allowed for sacrifice, and to eat the food so prepared, Can any unbiassed person then, say, that 7 hours and half would have sufficed, to perform all this? Would it not rather have been regarded as a mockery, to be directed to " *take needful refreshment, as the night* required;" when the whole night must have passed, before it was attainable?

But the *event* clearly shews, that the place was not very far off, as the provisions arrived early; for it follows " that " they arrived in large quantities from *Troy;* oxen and " sheep, with store of wine and bread : and they gathered " much fuel." And that subsequently, they sat watching " their numerous fires, *till day break.*[k]"

So that these transactions did not employ the *whole* night: since after their supper, they sat watching their fires during *the remainder of the night.* It can hardly be conceived then, that the provisions came from a place more than 7 miles distant.

Nor does this arrangement at all contradict the fact of the Trojan camp fires, on the *Throsmos*, illuminating the lofty front of Troy; so as to render it visible to Agamemnon, in the Grecian camp, or fleet, at the distance of 4 miles: and doubtless more applicable to a distance of 4, than of 7

[k] Iliad, lib. viii. v. 545 *et seq.*: Cowper, v. 625.

miles.[l] For, referring to the compartments N°. I. and II. of the Map, it will appear, that if Troy extended into the Plain, opposite to the *Tumulus* taken for that of *Myrinna*, its front, or at least, the upper part of its edifices, might well be visible to Agamemnon; especially if his tent, as may be supposed, was placed on a mound, thrown up for the purpose, as was the ancient practice: or on his ascending a ship, as he did that of Ulysses, when he harangued the army.[m]

Nor does this view of the City, from the Camp, although it may seem to imply a view of the camp from the city, involve any absurdity in the act of sending Polites to *reconnoitre* on a former occasion. For although the city might have been seen from a small elevation in the camp, yet the army, standing on a low beach, might not be visible from the city: or if seen, the position of its front might have been too oblique to distinguish particulars. But at the *Tumulus* at the ancient conflux of the Mender and Bounarbashi Rivers, the front of the Grecian army would have been clearly open to the view; so as to ascertain whether the

[l] " For cast he but his eye toward the plain
" Of Ilium, there, astonish'd, he beheld
" The city *fronted with bright fires ;* and heard
" Pipes, and recorders, and the hum of war."—

(Lib. x. v. 10, *et seq.* : Cowper, v. 11.)

And in viii. v. 557,
——————————— " those fires
" In prospect all of Troy."— (Cowper, v. 643.)

It must be owned that these descriptions do not seem to refer to a city at more than 7 miles off.

[m] Iliad, lib. viii. v. 222 : Cowper, v. 256.

division of Achilles marched with the main body. (See above, page 107).

From all the above circumstances, taken together, one cannot help believing, that the ancient City of TROY, or ILIUM, stood somewhere in the quarter, between Atchekui and Kalifatli: which site must also have included, that of the *Iliean* village. But no traces of either, are recognised in these times; and even the precise site of the *Iliean* Village, is as little known at present, as that of *Ancient Ilium,* in the days of Demetrius. And indeed Lucan appears to be justified in saying, that the ruins of Troy had themselves perished before his day. Nor is it at all wonderful: since there was so vast a demand for materials for the building of other cities in its neighbourhood.[n]

---

[n] It would appear, that some persons have expected, from the expression of Virgil, Æn. ii. v. 21, that Troy should have stood *opposite* to *Tenedos.* But they are said to be *in sight* of each other, only.

SECTION II.

CONCERNING THE PLACES OF THE FIELDS OF BATTLE, &c. &c.

Alexander's Admiration of the ILIAD, *seems to shew that he thought the Narrative consistent : which it could not have been, had* Troy *occupied the site of* Bounarbashi—*Remark of M.* Heyne—*First Battle, in front of the* Scæan *Gate— The fortifying of the Camp and Fleet, a probable Transaction* —SECOND *Battle, in the middle space, between* Troy *and the* Camp—*The* Greeks *suffer a defeat ; and shelter themselves within their Fortification* — *The* Trojans *encamp close to them, on the* Throsmos ; *and threaten an attack, the next Morning*—*Night Adventure of* Ulysses *and* Diomed, *in the Valley of* Thymbra—THIRD *Battle, on the* Throsmos ; *desperate, and long continued ; with alternate success—The Rampart assaulted, and carried by the* Trojans : *but they are finally driven out by* Patroclus, *who is afterwards slain before* Troy ; *and the* Trojans *regain their Station on the* Throsmos—*Errors of modern Authors, respecting the Position of the Monument of* Ilus—*Mr.* Pope *makes five Battles of the warfare of this day*—Achilles *having returned to the War, the* FOURTH, *and last Battle is fought on the* Throsmos : *the* Trojans *are totally defeated, and driven into their City ; and* Hector *slain.*

AFTER what has been said in the preceding Sections, it is by no means difficult to fix the places of the different fields of battle ; provided that the above positions of the Tombs of *Ilus* and *Myrinna*, as well as the courses of the *Scamander* and *Simoïs*, are admitted.

Homer having given a *real field of action*, it may be supposed that he meant to deliver as truths, the *general movements* made in and about it. And it may therefore be concluded, that, after the poem is stripped of its agency of gods ; and of the poetical embellishments of human actions, that the marches and battles, and the arrangements respecting the fleet and rampart, are to be received as *general truths :* and that the Topography is in unison with the Narrative.°

Alexander is said to have been a passionate admirer of the Iliad : and he had an opportunity of deciding on the spot, how far the Topography was consistent with the Narrative. Had he been shewn the site of Bounarbashi, for that of Troy, he would probably have questioned the fidelity, either of the historical part of the poem, or of his guides. It

---

° Not but that the chain of transactions has doubtless been subjected to such an arrangement as would best suit the train of causes and consequences.

The Poet might find it necessary to carry one of his principal personages by a circuitous route, in order to bring about a catastrophe, after his own manner. It may be said, for instance, that Nestor (lib. xi. v. 596.) in carrying Machaon, wounded, from the *left* of the field, past the tent of Achilles on the *right,* in his way to the *centre* of the Greek camp, whilst there were other gates nearer to the centre, by which he might have entered ; (Lib. vii. v. 339) appears to be done, in violation of probability : and that, for the purpose of drawing the attention of Achilles. For had Nestor entered the camp, by the *direct* road, Achilles would not have seen him : nor, of course, would have sent out Patroclus ; whose sally forth, produced the chain of events, that led to the *grand catastrophe.* But after all, there may have been reasons for making the *detour :* although they do not appear in the Poem.

is not within credibility, that a person of so correct a judgment as Alexander, could have admired a poem, which
contained a long history of military details, and other transactions, that could not, physically, have had an existence.
What pleasure could he receive, in contemplating as subjects
of history, events that could not have happened? Yet he
did admire the Poem; and therefore must have found the
Topography consistent: that is, Bounarbashi, surely, was
not shewn him for Troy!

M. Heyne justly observes, that " to a person who knew
" the Topography of the country, in the days of Homer,
" nothing would be represented, which he would have recog-
" nised, and declared to be false, and erroneous; else the
" effect of the Poem would be lost." (Edin. Trans. Vol. IV.
p. 79.)—" The Poet indeed is not to be a geographer; but
" he must not feign any thing which contradicts the first
" glance of nature; or clashes with the known accounts of
" the Topography of the Country." (page 78).

Places of the Fields of Battle.

THE FIRST battle was fought *before* Troy: the Trojan
army being marshalled at the Tomb of Myrinna, or Batiæa,
which was said to stand in the Plain, " *in front of Ilium ;*"[p]
and so near the *Scæan* Gate, that the persons of the Grecian
chiefs could be distinguished.[q] It is said that this battle was

[p] Iliad, lib. ii. v. 811 : Cowper, v. 939.   See Nº. II. of the Map.
[q] Lib. iii. v. 144, *et seq.* : Cowper, 179.
This is doubtless to be regarded as a poetical fiction, though a very agreeable

fought in the middle Plain, between the Rivers *Scamander* and *Simoïs.*[r] Juno and Minerva, who visit the field, descend at the place of meeting of the two rivers : and it is probable that the Poet meant to set them down very near to the place of action. One may therefore conclude, that this must refer to the *upper* conflux, near Kalifatli; where the Shimar is said by Mr. Carlyle, to fall into the Mender, during the seasons when it is *swoln*. But the place of the conflux in ancient times, however, is not clearly described; although one may comprehend its general position.

We should therefore place the field of the first battle, between the Village of Kalifatli, and the Tumulus above it; taken by Mr. Gell for that of *Myrinna*. The battle ends, only in the *seventh* Book : after which, the Greeks fortify their camp and fleet.[s] The Reader is again referred to the compartment, N°. II. of the Map.

Here it may be proper to say a word, respecting the fact of the existence of the rampart, or wall, at the fleet; since so important a part of the warfare happened there. Some have thought the story to be an *absolute fiction*. But why? Could any measure be more necessary; more easy of execution, since it was performed in a single day; or more probable, from both these causes? It was what would be styled in modern war, *a light field work;* such as are hastily thrown up, on pressing emergencies.

one. For, as the Army of Troy would doubtless occupy the ground *nearest* to Troy ; that of Greece must necessarily have been *more distant* from the town, and consequently too far off, to admit of any nice discriminations of persons. The Tumulus, however, may have been very near to Troy.

[r] Lib. vi. v. 3.   [s] Lib. vii. v. 337, *et seq.*

s

The ancients were in the habit of fortifying their fleets, when *drawn up* on the shore; of which, frequent instances occur in history.   Nearchus did so, repeatedly.   At the *Port of Alexander*, he built a stone wall, and remained 24 days.   And at the *Anamis* River, he made a *double* rampart and ditch.   So far from considering the wall, as a fiction, it should rather be regarded as one of the most probable facts in the Poem.[t]

The ease, with which it was forced by Hector, proves its defective construction, from the hasty manner of executing it.   A part, on the *left*, was *very low*; and advantage was taken of it.[u] Possibly, the soil there, was more wet and marshy than in other places; so that they soon *came to water*; and therefore could not easily get earth enough to raise it higher.   (Surely, these are all probable circumstances.)   And that the whole should have been obliterated, before the days of Homer, is not at all wonderful.[x]   The surge of the sea, alone, in rough weather (it being exposed to N. W. winds) considering how very near the margin it must have been, was sufficient to produce the effect, in the course of a very few ages.

It may be remarked, that the present course of the *lower*

[t] Thucydides reasons on it, as on a supposed fact. " If (says he) they had not been superior in the field, they could not have fortified their camp." (Lib. i.)

[u] Iliad, lib. xiii. v. 681, *et seq.*
———— The gallies there
Of Ajax and Protesilaüs stood
Updrawn above the hoary deep ; the wall
Was there of *humblest structure.* ————   (Cowper, v. 809, *et seq.*)

[x] The interval is supposed to be somewhat short of 300 years.

Shimar, from the mouth of the Valley of Thymbrek, to the Mender; occupies nearly the line, which we should assign to the exterior of the rampart. (See N°. I.)

The SECOND battle ʸ seems to have been fought in the same Plain, though not so near Troy: but rather perhaps about midway between it and the fleet; as both parties appear to have sallied forth, about the same time. The battle was soon decided; the Greeks retiring to their wall for shelter, very early; closely pursued and harassed by the Trojans; who, in the end, formed their camp on the *Throsmos*, or Plain, above the beach, opposite to the wall, and ranging with the sepulchre of ILUS. (See N°. II)

This position was taken (as we have before remarked) with a view to prevent the Greeks, had they been so determined, from escaping with their fleet, during the night. The *right* of the Trojan line, including the auxiliaries, extended *within* the entrance of the Valley of *Thymbra*, and terminated on the sea coast; or rather on the *Bay*; as the sea must *then* have entered much deeper into the land, than at present; and probably touched on the mouth of the Valley of *Thymbra*.ᶻ

And here it must have been, that the night adventure of Ulysses and Diomed took place; when the *Thracian* Chief, *Rhesus*, was slain, and his horses carried off.

ʸ Iliad, lib. viii. v. 60 : Cowper, v. 66.

ᶻ Iliad, lib. x. v. 426, *et seq.* : Cowper, v. 488. It is said that " The *Carians* were posted by the *sea* : and on the skirts of *Thymbra*, the *Mæonians, Phrygians, Lydians,* and *Mysians.*"—and " farthest removed of all, on the utmost border of the camp, were the *Thracians*: newly arrived." These were doubtless the Thracians of the opposite *Chersonesus*.

Their track must have been along the beach, in front of the ditch, towards the Vale of *Thymbra :* so that the spy, *Dolon,* who came immediately from Hector's head quarters at Ilus' Monument, and was bending towards those of Agamemnon, in the centre of the fleet,[a] was very soon intercepted by the Grecian chiefs.   The *Thracians* lay *" the most remote of all,* on the *borders of the Trojan camp ;"* and *beyond the Lycians,* &c. who were *" on the skirts of Thymbra."*[b] Hence we should place the Thracians *within* the *Valley* of *Thymbra ;* and of course, beyond the bed of the *Scamander.*   Dolon says, *" if ye wish to penetrate the host."* &c. : so that to reach the Thracians, whose plunder had allured them, it is implied that Ulysses and Diomed *penetrated* the *first line* of troops ; which, according to Dolon, being composed of auxiliaries, were careless of the general welfare, and were all asleep. (See also page 90.)

The THIRD battle was on the ground of the just mentioned encampment of the Trojan army, which ranged close to the Tomb of Ilus, along the *Throsmos ;* and parallel to the Grecian rampart.[d]

> " Opposite, on the rising-ground appear'd
> " The Trojans."—(Lib. xi. v. 56: Cowper, v. 68.)

This third battle was the most desperate, and long con-

---

[a] Iliad, lib. x. v. 326 : Cowper, v. 375.

[b] The *Valley* of *Thymbra,* not the Town, or the Temple, is to be understood. From circumstances, as well as from the shortness of the time they were absent, it is probable that the Thracians were not far up the Valley.   Nor ought they indeed to have been, as they formed a part of the Trojan army.

[c] Iliad, lib. x. v. 422 : Cowper, v. 482.   [d] See above, page 102.

tested, of any in the Iliad : it lasting from day-light till noon, (See above, page 120, *et seq.*) ; when the Trojans gave way, and were pursued " *through the middle Plain, beside the sepul-* " *chre of Ilus, towards the fig tree,*"—seeking to regain the town.* Then, the chance of war suddenly turning against the Greeks, they were driven back to the front of their forti-fication : and the Trojans took a position on their old ground, the *Throsmos,* and near to the Sepulchre of Ilus : for Paris wounded Diomed and others from behind a *pillar* or *column* of it, during the battle that followed, near the rampart. But the act of retiring of the Greeks, *within* their fortification, is not noticed. " *Podalirius in the field, maintains sharp conflict* *with the sons of Troy,*" in lib. xi. v. 832 : but in xii. v. 40, they are said to be " *within their fleet immured.*" ᶠ (Cowper, xi. v. 1013, and xii. v. 48.)

Then follows, in the same Book, the assault of the ram-part, on the left—and afterwards, much fighting, both *within*

ᵉ Iliad, lib. xi. v. 166. Here it might seem as if the Sepulchre of Ilus, lay *far* in the rear of the Trojans ; but the fact, as is shewn, in page 82 *et seq.* is, that it could not be far from the sea beach. And, on the other hand, the fig tree, or Erineus, was close to Troy.

One would have thought that a very slight attention to the warfare at the ships, would have enabled any person to avoid the errors that have been com-mitted, on this occasion. Mr. Pope has placed the Monument of Ilus, *nearer* to the *town,* than to the *ships;* although the Trojan camp was close to it, and also *within hearing of the voices* of the people in the Grecian camp. (See above, page 84.

And in the notes to Cowper, we find: " This tomb was equi-distant from Troy, and the camp of the Greeks."

How was it possible to err so widely !

ᶠ The Poet no doubt meant that this, as well as many other minor circum-stances, should be taken or granted.

and *without* it, during the succeeding four Books (i. e. the xiii. xiv. xv. and part of the xvi.th :) when Patroclus, at the head of the Myrmidons, finally drove out the Trojans, and pursued them home to Troy. There he is slain; and the Greeks are again beaten back to their wall (lib. xvii. and xviii.); behind which they retire (a second time the same day,) whilst the Trojans, a *third* time, occupy their old position on the *Throsmos;* as appears by the transactions of the next day. (Lib. xx. v. 3.)

———— " opposite
" The Trojans on the rising ground appear'd;"

whilst the Greeks under Agamemnon, Ajax, and Achilles, were marshalled at their fleet.

So that, after this long fought and eventful day, both parties, at or before sunset, were in possession of the same ground, which they had respectively occupied in the morning.

Mr. Pope has divided the transactions of *this day*, into no less than 5 battles.[s] He reckons, properly enough, the THIRD battle to have been that, fought on the *rising ground*, opposite to the ships, in the morning. But then, he makes a FOURTH battle, of the attack of the wall; the fighting at the ships a FIFTH; the attack made by Patroclus, a SIXTH; and finally a SEVENTH, for the body of Patroclus. How far this mode of arrangement is proper, may be doubted. It may rather be apprehended, that *five* battles were never fought in one day, by the same individual parties : and that these are rather *separate attacks*, constituting altogether one battle.[h]

[s] In the arguments prefixed to the Books of the Iliad, in his translation.
[h] The Author is much gratified, at finding that in this opinion, as well as in

The *last* battle, and in our mode of arrangement, the FOURTH (the EIGHTH of Mr. Pope), is that, in which Achilles, after his reconciliation with Agamemnon, first appears as a warrior in the field: for hitherto, he has taken no part in the military transactions. (lib. xx.) Accordingly, the Trojans were attacked once more in their old position; from whence they were driven across, or into *the Scamander*, (which seems to have become swoln at the instant, and to have overwhelmed multitudes of them); and then along the Plain of Troy, till the remainder took shelter in the city. HECTOR alone remains without; and meets his death from ACHILLES.

most others, respecting the present subject, he has the happiness of agreeing with the learned HEYNE.

[See the Edinb. Phil. Trans. Vol. IV. p. 88, Literary Class.]

SECTION III.

CONCERNING THE TUMULUS OF HECTOR.

The Funeral of Hector *probably took place* without, *and not* within, *the City of* TROY—*Several* Tumuli *near* Atchekui, *not known to M. de Chevalier.—The* Tumulus *of Hector probably formed of* Earth, *not of* stones ; *the stones being employed only in covering the funereal urn.*

MUCH has been said concerning the position and nature of the *tumulus* of Hector : whether it was situated *within* the *Pergama* of Troy, or at some distance *without* the city : and whether it was composed of earth, or of stones.

Certainly, when it is learnt from the transactions during the truce, that so vast a mass of wood, as required nine days to cut down and to transport,[i] was brought from *Ida*, to form a pile for burning the body of Hector ; one can hardly reconcile to prudence, the measure of firing it, in a mass, within the circuit of a populous city ! On *this* ground alone, one can suppose no other, than that it was placed without the city.

Concerning the exact import of the words, in which the description of the tomb is couched, it appears that the learned themselves are not agreed : some believing that a *Tumulus of Stones* is intended ; others, that stones were *laid*

[i] Iliad, lib. xxiv, v. 778 : Cowper, v. 983.

over the Pit, or Sepulchre, only ; and the *Tumulus* raised of earth, as in other cases.

The author, of course, has no pretensions to obtrude his opinion in this matter, in respect of the import of those words. *A Tumulus* of stones is certainly found, on the hill over Bounarbashi, the supposed *Pergama* of Troy ; and great stress is laid on this circumstance, as if it was decisive of the position of Troy. This, perhaps, is assuming too much ; especially as there are other *Tumuli,* between the *Mender* and the *Shimar* Rivers. For there are two *Tumuli* at about ⅓ of a mile to the eastward of Atchekui (the supposed *Kalli-colone.*) One of these is named by Mr. Carlyle, *Kana Tepe;* by Capt. Francklin, *Anai Tepe;* and said by him to mean "*The Tumulus of Stones.*" [k] The other lies at a small distance to the westward of the first; the road to Bounarbashi passing between them. And there is yet a *third,* distinctly remarked only by Mr. Carlyle and Mr. Gell, at ⅔ of a mile to the N. W. of Atchekui, or midway between it and the supposed hill of the *Pagus Iliensium.*

This latter *Tumulus* is named *Mal Tepe*[1] by Mr. Carlyle; and as seen from the Hill of Bounarbashi, in Mr. Gell's XXXI st Plate (for it is doubtless the same) appears in a bold situation, near the *brow* of the elevated land, that bounds the Plain to the north, between Atchekui and the supposed Hill of the *Pagus.*[m]

[k] Page 13 of his Tour.

[1] *Mal-tepé* is also the name of a small hill in the road between Constantinople and *Nicomedia,* near the sea-coast. Its signification is said to be "*Hill of Riches.*"

[m] It is seen over the top of the *ploughed hill,* on the right of the Plate, N°. XXXI. For the places of these *Tumuli* in the Map, see N°. I.

T

On a subject so interesting to the feelings, as every particular concerning Hector must be; where a whole city goes
forth to do honour to the remains of their defender and
guide : one may be allowed to go somewhat more into detail,
with a view to enquire, which is the most probable, from
the words of the Poet, that the Monument was *within* or
without the city; and whether composed of *earth*, or of
stones?

The Poet says, (lib. xxiv. v. 778, *et seq*.)ᵃ " Priam ordered
the Trojans to go, and convey wood, towards the city, without
fear of any ambush or onset from the Greeks. The Trojans
yoked their oxen and mules to their wains, and assembled
themselves before the city.   Nine days they were employed
in collecting a huge pyre of wood : and on the tenth morning, with many tears, they carried forth the body of bold
Hector ; and having placed it on the summit, set fire to the
pile. When the next morning appeared, the Trojans again
assembled, and completely extinguished the pyre with black
wine. Hector's brothers and companions then collected the
white bones, bedewing them with their tears. The bones,
involved in a covering of soft purple, they inclosed in a
golden coffer, which they deposited quickly in the hollow
of a deep pit, which they covered completely a-top with
huge stones, and then hastily raised a mound or monument
around it : the watchmen observing on all sides, lest the
Greeks should rush in, before the work was completed.
Having raised the mound, they returned again [to the city];
and then assembling in great numbers, feasted in Priam's
palace."ᵒ

ᵃ Translated by Dr. Gillies.

ᵇ Dr. Chandler also read this passage in the same way : " The relics were

To us, these descriptions seem to apply to a transaction *without*, and not *within*, the walls of a populous and closely built capital. The " *carrying forth* " of the body, attended, as is implied, by the general population, could only have been into a *large open space* : and where could it be carried *forth to*, but to a place on the *outside* of the city ? The population of a large city, is assembled *around a particular spot* : how could a sufficient space be found within the city ; even if the difficulty of avoiding the danger of fire, from such an enormous mass of fuel, could have been got over ?

Again, the stones appear to have been used only for covering the *grave ;* and not in the *piling* of the *Tumulus.* They were *huge*, that is, suited to the intended purpose of securing the urn : but the *piling in haste* seems to refer to *earth*, rather than *stones.*ᴾ Moreover, it seems to have been customary in those times, to employ stones, or masonry, about the sepulchre itself, but to cover the whole with earth.

In respect of there being a number of persons on the watch, it may be observed, that had the transaction been within the city, with its whole population abroad in the streets, what need was there of greater precaution than usual ? The spies or centinels, one would rather conclude, were placed in relays between Troy and the Grecian camp, to be ready to warn the people employed *without* the city,

---

" *secured* in a pit by laying *many large stones over them :* which done, the " Barrow was thrown up hastily, and the party *returned to the city.*" [MSS.]

ᴾ Obviously : because in most situations, loose stones, in such quantities, are not so readily obtained in one spot, as earth ; which, in most situations, may be dug out, easily. But they might also have employed such loose stones as were to be had.

to return for its defence, if necessary.   And admitting that the *Pagus Iliensium* was the *Pergama* of Troy, and *Mal Tepe*, the Tumulus in question, there would have been great need of warning; since it is situated $\frac{2}{3}$ of a mile, beyond the *Pagus*, in respect of the Grecian camp; and the view of the approach obstructed by intermediate hills.

We shall close our remarks on this article by observing, that a *Tumulus* of stones, or rubbish, would indeed have suited the circumstances of a people, who had not the power given them by a truce, to go forth, for the purpose of collecting fuel from distant forests; for performing the rites of sepulture; and even for building the tomb.[q] But in possession of this power, would they not also avail themselves of the opportunity of raising such a monument as was proper to the occasion; and especially, when the customary mode of executing it, was within their power, and apparently, the most expeditious?

[q] Iliad, lib. xxiv. v. 666: Cowper, v. 832.

SECTION IV.

CONCLUSION.

That the Mender *and* Shimar *Rivers appear to be the* Scamander *and* Simoïs *of* HOMER : *and the space between
them, of course, the* SCENE *of the* ILIAD—*That the Hill of
Atchekui, appears to answer to the* Kalli-colone.—*That the
distance of Bounarbashi, considered as* TROY, *is much too
great, from the Sea, to accord with the history of the warfare
in the Poem—That the Stream of* Bounarbashi *has no resemblance, in point of Character, to the* Scamander *of Homer—
That the two Springs, pointed out at Bounarbashi, afford no
contrast in their temperature ; as the history requires—And,
finally, that the* CITY *of* TROY *stood in a* Plain ; *but that
the entire site of Bounarbashi is* hilly.

T HE Author trusts, that, by means of the notices collected
from different quarters; but more particularly from Demetrius of *Scepsis,* he has impressed a conviction on the mind
of the reader, that the Plain of Troy is NOT where M. de
Chevalier has placed it ; but on the opposite, or eastern
shore of the Mender : as also, that there is no reason why
the authority of Demetrius should be questioned, in this
matter.

It is hoped, that it has also been shewn,

I. That the SCAMANDER, being the principal river in
Homer's description, and having the character of a powerful

and impetuous *torrent*, is recognised in the MENDER River, which bears the like character: and which is joined on the east side, by a *lesser* river, of much the same description, named SHIMAR, or SIMORES: and answering to the SIMOIS of Homer. Whence, we have the MENDER and SHIMAR, for the SCAMANDER and SIMOÏS.

II. That the space between these rivers, is *the real Scene of the Iliad*, according to Demetrius; who describes it, as being divided, lengthwise, by a ridge of high land, into two unequal plains; of which, the largest, and in which most of the battles were fought, was on the side towards the *Scamander:* and such a ridge of high land is actually found; with the widest division of the plain towards the *Mender.*

III. That within the just mentioned space, between the two rivers, and at 30 stadia from *New Ilium,* towards the East and Mount Ida, was the Village of the *Ilieans;* supposed to stand on a part of the site of ANCIENT TROY. And at 10 stadia beyond that, or 40 from New Ilium, on a continuation of the same line of direction, was the *Kalli-colone,* or *beautiful hill,* described by Demetrius. And that, an insulated, conical hill, known by the name of Atchekui, from a village on its summit, has been recognised by certain travellers, as agreeing, generally, in situation and description, with the *Kalli-colone.* But there are not found any tokens by which the site of the Village of the *Ilieans* can be ascertained.

That by the history of the transactions in the Poem, it appears, that the *Kalli-colone* (as well as the City of Troy) should have stood in the space between the *Scamander* and the *Simoïs:* and the hill of Atchekui does really stand between the Mender and the Shimar.

IV. That *Tumuli* are found within the same Plain : one of which, from its position, may be taken for that of *Myrinna* or *Batiœa ;* and others for those of *Ilus* and *Æsyetes.* But no *Tumulus whatsoever* is found in the *opposite* Plain ; or that assumed by M. de Chevalier, for the Plain of Troy.

V. That the distance of Bounarbashi (considered as Troy) from the supposed site of the Grecian camp and fleet, is such, as to be utterly irreconcilable to the history of the transactions; since large armies, must, in that case, not only have marched, in order of battle, and very often, fighting by the way; over 30, or more miles of ground, in 7 hours and half, or less; but also, within the same space of time, the Trojans must have assaulted and taken the Grecian wall. But that the story is consistent, if referred to the site of the Village of the *Ilieans;* which was supposed by Demetrius, to stand on a part of the site of Troy.

VI. That the promptitude with which the cattle, sheep, and other provisions, were brought into the camp of Hector whilst watching the Greeks, to prevent their expected embarkation and flight, fully proves the vicinity of the City of Troy to that Camp; whilst, from Bounarbashi, the provisions could not have reached them, and also have been brought into use, during the interval of time assigned in the history.

VII. That the Bounarbashi River, taken by M. de Chevalier, for the *Scamander* of HOMER, is a stream scarcely twenty feet in width, and three in depth; and being supplied by equal and perennial springs, rising in the Plain ; and having a course of eight miles only ; cannot become at times a

furious torrent, like the *Scamander* of Homer, which was derived from the eastern quarter of Mount *Ida,* and had a
capacity in its bed, sufficient to receive fighting parties; as
well as to allow the Trojan fugitives to hide themselves
That the expression of Homer, respecting the TWO SOURCES
of this river, before the *Scœan* Gate, appears to be subject to
different interpretations: that is, to mean either the HEADS
OF a River: or ADJUNCTS TO a River.   Moreover, that the
Bounarbashi River does by no means accord in description
with the *Scamander* of Demetrius, in respect of the actual
geography: for this latter received into its bed, the River
Andrius, from the quarter of *Carasena*: but the Bounarbashi
River receives no adjunct stream whatsoever; nor could it,
from the quarter of *Carasena,* because the course of the
Mender interposes.

VIII. That the lower part of the course of the *Scamander*
of Homer, intervened between the Camp of the Greeks and
the City of Troy; as appears by more than one circumstance
in the history of the Poem: but the course of the River of
Bounarbashi, does not intervene, whether Troy be placed at
the Village of Bounarbashi, or at the supposed site of the
Iliean village.

IX. That there is no hill whatsoever, in the Plain fixed
on by M. de Chevalier, that can be taken for the *Kalli-
colone:* a very important fact.

X. That the Springs of Bounarbashi, howsoever imposing
in respect of their appearance and accompaniments,[r] do
not present any *contrast,* in point of temperature; as must
surely be looked for, from the description of the springs,

[r] See Mr. Gell's Troy, page 74, 75.

in Homer: but are *alike cold.* That there are not TWO, ONLY, but a considerable number of them; and all of the same temperature; which appears to be 5 or 6 degrees above the *mean temperature* of the atmosphere. That as Demetrius, who lived near the spot, *could not find the Springs intended by Homer;* and who could not but have known such remarkable ones, as those of Bounarbashi; one must conclude that he looked elsewhere, for the springs designed by Homer: and that the cold spring mentioned by Strabo, as one of the two, must have been in a different situation.

XI. And lastly, That as Ancient Troy is said to have been " *reared in the Plain,*" one must conclude that the body of the city stood generally on flat ground; although it contained a *Pergama,* or citadel on a hill; and consequently a slope of ground, up to it. But the site fixed on by M. de Chevalier, between Bounarbashi Village and the River Mender, is *entirely hilly.*

U

ADDENDA.

I. Refers to page 60, note h.

It is not improbable, that the state in which Doctor Clarke saw the bed of the Shimar, was after a recent flood. See above, page 39, Note.

II. Refers to page 61, line 6.

Mr. Gell has obligingly communicated the following remark, which was omitted in his book.

" I know of little, interesting, between the Ford of the Mender and Kalifatli, except that before you reach Kalifatli, going northward, *a bank of sand, or earth, with trees or bushes on the top, is seen on the other, or west side of the Mender.* This may have been only thrown up by the water, but it brought to my recollection the Tomb of Ilus, the Mound of the Plain, Myrinna, &c. &c. At a guess, it lies about East from Erkessi-kui.

III. Refers to page 63.

Mr. Gell states, that he saw the smoke, or steam, over the source nearest Bounarbashi [the reputed warm spring];

and that the water felt warm to the touch. The other spring, which was of the like temperature, at the mouth, did not send up any steam from its reservoir.

IV. Refers to page 80. Note n : Omitted in place.

It may reasonably be supposed, that the Greeks, at this period, were reduced to half their original number; that is, to nearly an equality with the Trojan army, in the field. For, besides the ordinary waste of an army, engaged in active warfare, they had suffered by the ravages of a pestilence.

V. Refers to page 86, line 18.

The Ancients do not pretend that the sea, in the time of Homer, came within 6 stadia of the *site* of New Ilium; which is only about a quarter of a mile higher up, than is expressed in the Map, Nº. II. So that even the Tumulus at Koum-kui, would still have been at some distance inland; and the one in question, much more than a mile and half.

VI. Refers to page 97.

" On the road between Koum-kevi, and the bridge of Koum-kale, manycavities are found, sometimes containing water, and generally pointing towards the Rhœteum Promontory. These have every resemblance to decayed channels; and if they did not originally convey the river to the sea, the use of them will not easily be discovered.

[Mr. Gell's Troy, p. 43.]

VII. Refers to page 100.

Mr. Gell says, " I cannot help thinking, that the Tumulus which I have named from *Ilus*, would have been opposite to that wing of the Grecian army commanded by Ajax; if the Scamander ever ran, as we both suppose, by Koum-kui. Also, supposing the Scamander to have taken that course, and to have bounded the Grecian camp, I cannot conceive a better position on any eminence, than the *Throsmos*, which I have recorded (that is, a hill nearly detached from the heights of Jenishehr, projecting into the Plain; and being the cause, which turned the stream of the river, towards the Rhœtean Promontory). And surely, there was no other place so proper for watching the Greeks."

[illegible] Refers to page 10.

Mr. Gell says, "I cannot help thinking, that the Turcoble hill I have named from him, would have been opposite to that wing of the Grecian army commanded by [illegible] of the commander [illegible], as we both suppose, be [illegible]. Also, supposing the commander to have taken that course and to have commanded the Grecian camp, I cannot conceive a better position on any emergency, than the [illegible], which I have recorded (that is, a hill nearly detached from the heights of Jerusalem projecting into the Plain), and being the cause, which turned the stream of the river towards the [illegible] Promontory. And surely there was no other place so proper for watching the Greeks."

INDEX.

A

X

Page

Of Mal Tepé, 137. Of Myrinna or Batiæa, 28, 40, 112. Of Patroclus, - 70
Tumuli, two discovered by Dr. Clarke, 40, 85, 107. None found in the Plain between the Mender and Bounarbashi Rivers, 143

Tymbrek. See Thymbrek.

U.

Udjek Tepé, not the Tumulus of Æsyetes, 106
Ulysses, his night ·adventure, in company with Diomed, 90, 91, 103, 131. Expresses his fears to Agamemnon, in the event of a precipitate retreat, - 103, 118

W.

Wall of the Greeks, observations on, 129, *et seq*. The fact of its construction, pro-

Page

bable, 130. Believed by Thucydides, 130. The Greeks retire within it, 131. Attacked and stormed by the Trojans, 133. Hastily constructed and imperfect, 130. Supposed line of its course, - - 131
Walpole, Mr. his route over Western and Southern Ida, - - 21
War of Troy, believed to have happened by Herodotus, Thucydides, the historians of Alexander, &c. &c. - 8, *et seq*.

X.

Xanthus, another name given by Homer to the Scamander, - 2, 93. 96
Xenophon, - - 20. 21. 25

Z.

Zeleia, at the eastern foot of Ida, 17, 25

London : Printed by W. Bulmer and Co. Cleveland-Row, St. James's.

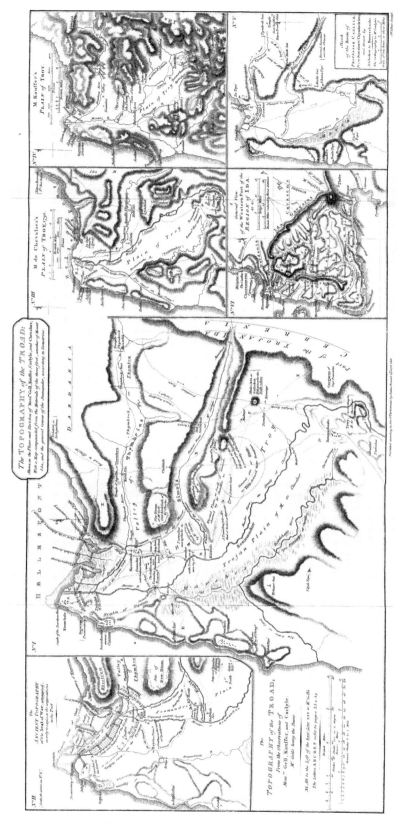

The material originally positioned here is too large for reproduction in this reissue. A PDF can be downloaded from the web address given on page iv of this book, by clicking on 'Resources Available'.

For EU product safety concerns, contact us at Calle de José Abascal, 56–1°,
28003 Madrid, Spain or eugpsr@cambridge.org.

www.ingramcontent.com/pod-product-compliance
Ingram Content Group UK Ltd.
Pitfield, Milton Keynes, MK11 3LW, UK
UKHW030855150625
459647UK00021B/2797